MANAGEMENT CONSULTANCY SERVICES FOR SMALL SCALE INDUSTRIES

Management Consultancy Services
for
Small Scale Industries
An Appraisal of Quality Dimensions

Dr. Ram Chandra Rai
Professor Finance & Investment
Railway Staff College
Vadodara

ANMOL PUBLICATIONS PVT. LTD.
NEW DELHI - 110 002 (INDIA)

ANMOL PUBLICATIONS PVT. LTD.
4374/4B, Ansari Road, Daryaganj
New Delhi - 110 002

Management Consultancy Services for Small Scale Industries

First Edition, 2000

ISBN 81-261-0695-6

PRINTED IN INDIA

Published by J.L. Kumar for Anmol Publications Pvt. Ltd., New Delhi - 110 002 and Printed at Tarun Offset Press, Delhi.

Contents

Preface

Small scale industry can play an important role in dispersal of national income and reducing unemployment, thereby improving the quality of life of the majority of the population of India. However, the fact remains that majority of the world's poor reside in India and their number is steadily increasing. Review of the performance of this sector indicates that more than 75 per cent of the units are not performing well due to number of problems both internal and external. Government of India initiated policy of economic reforms in 1991 and it includes liberalisation and globalisation. The increased competition due to the policy of dereservation of the items earlier reserved for SSIs, has made the situation worst for this sector and it can hardly survive unless it professionalises its management. Literature survey indicates that mismanagement is the prime internal cause for bad performance which has side effects on all other areas. It is also established that majority of small entrepreneurs lack required entrepreneurial and managerial traits. Also due to weak financial resource base they can hardly engage management graduates on full time basis to meet their own managerial inadequacies. As such prime facie they should depend upon external part time assistance to solve their management problems.

There are about 15000 management consultants in India, mostly concentrated in the metros and other bigger and capital cities. However, taking into account poor performance of small scale industrial sector, it appears that either management consultants are not able to cope with the real management consultancy demand of this sector or their services are too costly or the quality of their services is poor and they are not able to solve the real management problems of the SSIs or there is lack of awareness on the part of small units about the usefulness of the management consultants. Therefore, it is high time that the real problems are ascertained and remedial action suggested.

Review of available literature indicates that hardly any worthwhile academic research has been done in this area in India. However, some government sponsored studies have been conducted by some institutions and some secondary information is available. Available literature indicates high degree of distrust between entrepreneurs of small scale units and the management consultants about the motives and capabilities of each other as the prime reason for low utilization of services of the consultants. However, the causes and full dimension of this perceived distrust has not been revealed. Therefore, a research study by the author attempted to probe this area in depth so as to find solutions to this problem.

This book aims at presenting the findings of research study conducted by the author to appraise the quality of management consultancy services available to Small Scale Industrial Units in India for the benefits of the academic fraternity and future researchers so as to facilitate further research in this area. The book has been divided into seven chapters. The first chapter presents the background of the research endeavour based on the research/studies already done including research methodology. The survey of literature on the works already done has been reviewed in the second chapter. Third, fourth and fifth, chapters present the analysis of the current feature and perceptions of supplier group, i.e. the management consultants and their association, user group i.e. SSI units and their associations the third group i.e. financial Institutions on various aspects of the quality of management consultancy services available to SSI units in India. The sixth chapter presents the analysis of the perception gaps of various respondent groups on relevant aspects. Finally the seventh chapter presents the conclusions drawn by the author on the basis of results of analysis, the inferences on the basis of the conclusions and his recommendations for improving the quality of management consultancy services and also its utilization by the Small Scale Industrial Units.

The research study as well as this book could not have been possible without co-operation and help from various quarters. I am really indebted to Dr. R.M. Srivastava, Dean Faculty of Management Studies, Banaras Hindu University (BHU), for his supervision and continuous guidance at each and every stage of this research. My special thanks are due to Shri Shreedhar Raghavan, Faculty Member of Management Development Institute, Gurgaon and a certified management consultant, Prof. S.K. Singh of Indian Institute of Management, Lucknow, Prof. K. Ramchandran of Indian Institute Management (IIM) Ahmedabad, Dr. R. Gopinath, Director CDC, New Delhi, Shri Brij Mohan, General Manager, SIDBI, Lucknow and A.K. Bhatanagar, Managing Director, U.P. Industrial Consultants Ltd. for the pain they have taken in guiding and helping me all through this research. I am also thankful to all the faculty members of Faculty of Management Studies, B.H.U. who have helped me by their frank opinions and views. My thanks are due to Managing Directors of the TCOs, Directors of SISIs productivity councils, SSI entrepreneurs, management consultants, officials of the banks who participated in this study without any hesitation. I am also thankful to the librarians of B.H.U., M.D.I., I.I.M Ahmedabad and Lucknow, Association of Indian Universities, American and British libraries and Japanese Cultural and Information Center, New Delhi.

North Eastern Railway Administration, especially Financial Advisor and Chief Account Officer, Smt. Sushma Pandey deserve special thanks for permitting the author to conduct this research along with his normal official engagements. Thanks are also due to the faculty members of Railway Staff College, Vadodara for their cooperation and the college administration especially Shri C.G. Bijlani, Principal, for allowing me to complete this work along with regular training activities. I cannot forget to thank my wife Kiran and sons Suyash and Shashvat for their patience in allowing me to devote time on this project on holidays and after office hours; the time which rightly belonged to them. Lastly I record my thanks to all those persons whose name could not be mentioned here for paucity of space but who have certainly helped me directly or indirectly in completion of this study.

Dr. Ram Chandra Rai

Vadodara

Abbreviations

TCOs	Technical Consultancy Organisations
SISIs	Small Industries Service Institutes
NPCs	National Productivity Councils
IMCI	Institute of Management Consultants of India
FIs	Financial Institutions

1

Introduction

1.1 BACKGROUND

1.1.1 Rationale for Small Scale Enterprises

Economic development of any country or region depends primarily upon peoples, ability, attitudes and their social and economical environment. Other non-human resources such as money, materials, machines and markets are secondary because their efficiency also depends upon human efficiency. The value system of some of the developing countries including India is anti-materialistic leading to lower manpower efficiency. Further economical development should facilitate peace and development of higher human faculties. Prosperity and uncontrolled expansion of needs of few at the cost of others leads to conflicts and its reduction leads to peace.

According to Buddhist philosophy, work has three basic functions i.e. utilisation and development of human faculties, overcoming of ego by joint enterprise and production of goods and services for existence. Work, if properly designed, improves the higher qualities of man and man without work becomes desperate and aggressive. This is basic cause of increasing crimes in society today. Poverty and unemployment are two most crucial problems coupled with lack of professionalism in almost all walks of life, India is facing today. According to the World Bank, though the percentage of poor in the overall population of India shows sign of decreasing. India has become the home of majority of world's poor and the rate of poverty alleviation in this country has dramatically slowed down in the 90's especially in the rural areas even when the national economy has grown at a much faster rate due to new policy of economic reforms initiated by Government of India. Also the gap between largest and poorest states and the better performing states is growing. Unless we are able to provide some means of livelihood to all those below poverty line, poverty can not be removed. Therefore, there is urgent need to plan for full employment. This strategy requires establishment of large number of work stations with affordable investment and appropriate technology. According to E.F. Scheumacher (194) small operations are normally eco-friendly. He is of the opinion that modern city man has reached such degree of anomity, social atomisation and spiritual isolation which is unprecedented in human history.

Gandhi also said that the poor can not be helped by mass production but production by masses. Mass production technology is normally capital intensive and also high energy based which is scarce but the system of production by masses mobilizes the priceless resource, i.e. men, clever brains and skillful hands. Secondly in most of the developing countries including India, 20% of the population is enjoying life at the cost of remaining 80 per cent. Also migration from villages to cities is leading to mutual poisoning i.e. destruction of social fabrics of the village due to migration of the adults and creation of slums and diseases due to overpopulation and resultant collapse of civic amenities in the cities. Therefore, work opportunities are to be created in rural areas mostly associated with agriculture and allied activities, based on simple technology, local skills and local markets. This can be best done by private small enterprises. Therefore, healthy development of small enterprises is essential for social peace and development of not only India but all those countries having socio- economic profile similar to India. Even the developed countries need well developed SSIs to support their economy.

1.1.2 Role of Management Consultants for small scale industrial units

Small size organisations require an approach on the part of consultants quite different from one needed for large size organisations. Since the SSI units are mostly one man show, the personal motivations/long term aspirations of SSI entrepreneurs have to be understood well, alongwith the need for multiskilling, whole brain (right and left) thinking, less emphasis on report writing, need for developing learning partner relationships, cost effective service and sustained support for a longer period. Though the analytical framework needed for small organisations may look simpler but the real problem may be the entrepreneur/owner himself. Therefore, small business consultation is not a cool and detached activity like one needed for larger organisations rather it is an emotionally charged activity required to be handled very carefully. The problems requiring solution through consultation may be related to growth of units, failure to meet the market needs or face the competition, skill gaps in the staff or house keeping problems. Against the present global trend of delayering in large size organisations for making them responsive and competitive, small organisations may be required to add layers to take care of the growth/expansions, place new management systems which may create tension/frustration in people. SSI units may like to know where they stand vis-à-vis their competitors. They may face the crisis of leadership, autonomy, control and red tape after having grown beyond a scale. Each phase need different approach to managing. However, like any other organisation, clarity of purpose, vision, values, measurement system and desired relationships is required here also. Consultants could assist SSI entrepreneurs in this exercise and also in identifying their problems, present stage of business, business path, the stage in which they may be entering now and how best they could prepare to work with and manage through SWOT (strength, weakness, opportunity and threats) analysis with the help of PEST (political, economic, social and technological trends) analysis. Consultant has to know as where the energy of people is focused, find out counter-productive relationships and has to take all people with him. SSI entrepreneurs being mostly lonely people normally seek trustworthy, well informed and experienced outside advisors who are capable of giving them access to best and most relevant learning, knowledge and new way of thinking. Therefore, attributes of mentorship are also required in consultants. SSI units being one man show, consultants have to use a lot of questioning and listening in order to understand the thinking process of the owner and has to adapt a process which can produce required learning, insight and lasting impact on the owner so that he may be ready to implement the recommendations of consultant. Useful conversation of consultant with clients double their brain power, increase the number of ways they could look at their problems and instills a sense of possibility. It is fact that SSI entrepreneurs are very egoist and will have to be fully involved in the entire consultation process to own the results of such exercise. Therefore, pre-formed solutions on the basis of consultant's own analysis without active involvement/consultation of the client may not work. The question answer session if well planned activates the thought process of the entrepreneur and his deep experience could be drawn to the surface, indirectly challenged, tested and changed. This exercise helps the client in internalising the new concepts, their relevance and benefits in the light of their own experience. Surprisingly the learning is more when the difference in the background (age, life stage, gender, experience etc.) of the consultant and client is more.

The personal agenda of the client rarely comes out in open unless his beliefs are threatened. Consultants have to do the brain mapping of clients and of their own. In many cases, like personal agenda of employees of big organisations the personal agenda of the owner may be in conflict with the business direction. However, the consultant has to learn to cope with the personal agenda of the client very carefully and find a business path which matches with it. The personal agenda could be funding life style, prove that he can do it, i.e. built a business and then move to next, derive excitement from new and risky tasks, love for an activity, sheer object of misappropriating govt. grants/loans or give employment to family members/friends/relatives etc. It is quite possible that he may not like to grow and may be interested in leading a peaceful life with all comforts. Every person has certain value system and goal in his life and SSI entrepreneurs are not exception to this. Since being the owner, he is in a position to influence course of entire unit, consultant has to understand these finer points of his personality. Once the personal agenda of the SSI owner is known, the consultant has to find out in an objective manner as what is best for the business. For this he must have lifetime perspective of the business under examination. Ideally by the time the consultation relationship comes to an end the client should have learned to think in different manner. However this may not be always possible due to deep rooted entrepreneurial inadequacies prevalent in the SSI sector. Since the cost of service is major consideration, common business performance workshops of non-competing SSI units in which owners could freely discuss about their personal agendas, needs of business and future of business etc. may be quite useful.

1.1.3 Existing status of knowledge

This study aims at appraisal of the quality of management consultancy services available to SSI units in India. In order to ascertain various dimensions of this activity including current status of knowledge, survey of related literature was conducted by the researcher and the results are reported in the second chapter. The results of literature survey about the user group (SSI units) and the supplier group (management consultants) can be summerised as under.

(a) On the side of user group, it can be said that development of SSI sector is inevitable for solving the twin problems of poverty and unemployment which are considered critical for peaceful development of society and improving the quality of life of millions of humans of not only India but other developing countries having socio-economic profile similar to India. There are about 3 million SSIs in India employing over 15 millions people but majority of them are not working well and sizable portion of them are sick/closed mainly due to management problems. Managerial incompetencies in the areas of project management, finance, resource utilisation and marketing coupled with technical incompetence are the major challenge before these units. It has been further reported that most of the SSI entrepreneurs lack basic entrepreneurial, managerial and technical skills required for successful conception, implementation and operation of SSI units.

(b) On the suppliers (management consultants) side it is seen that there are around 15000 consultants in India but majority of them are technical/project consultants. The basic features of consultancy profession considered relevant for this study have been reported be as under.

(i) Basic features of consultancy profession at the global level are existence of strategy, traditional general management, accounting, information technology and human relations consultants, faster annual growth (20%) of this profession, lack of effective quality controls mechanism but better in developed countries than developing countries, general unwillingness on the part of consultants to be regulated by their professional association/ institutes, general confusion about scope of management consultancy with strategy consultants disowning accountants and all disowning recruiters, demand for specialists with general aptitudes as consultants, reputation purely based on quality of service/feedback of the customers, mergers, large size consultancy firms in the developed countries as against smaller firms in developing countries and the major areas of consultation being franchise, public sector, local governments, IT, strategy formulation and review, organisational change and development and productivity studies besides traditional business consultancy.

(ii) Since this study concerns itself basically with the quality dimensions of management consultancy for SSI units, it was considered worthwhile to survey the related literature and the review reveals that quality dimensions include desirable personal characteristics of consultants such as time consciousness, in-depth knowledge of the field along with urge to update and adopt to changes, ability to take objective and integrated view, creativeness and innovation, ability to train and impart knowledge, entrepreneurship, vision and participate style, ability to resolve conflict, reliability and optimism for improvement, ability to work as neutral participant observer, belief in human potential, populist tendency and ability to unearth hidden motives of the client, problem solving ability, ability to sell and market and diversified skills for stable income; effectiveness of the selection process mostly based on past track records; dimensions of consultation process, i.e. existence of diagnostic theory to identify the real management problems of the client, extents of consultant's involvement (styles), ability to identify the forces for and against change, clear phasing of the consultation process, convincing the client that he needs change and empowerment of the clients; clarity of terms and condition of the consultancy contract, ability of client in identification of need for consultation, selection of proper consultant and optimal utilisation of consultant; degree and quality of consultant-client relationship, quality of implementation strategy, quality control mechanism, focused market segment, nature of engagement and size of consultancy organisation. Therefore, it was thought essential to focus on these aspects during the field research.

(iii) The major problems of consultants are mistrust between the consultant and client, lack of professionalism of the entrepreneurs and considering expenditure on consultancy as waste, lower payment capacity of SSIs, acute shortage of good quality consultants, low demand for consultancy, lack of data on consultancy needs and demand, very few consultants serving SSI units due to viability problems, frequent changes in the management of the client organisation, absence of survey of the feedback of the customers on quality of service, lack of willingness to be controlled by their associations/institutes, use of outdated management concepts by consultants, absence of proper training and development of consultants, misunderstanding between consultants and clients due to vague consultancy contracts, lack of involvement of clients, mishandling of assignments by junior consultants due to lack of proper supervision by senior consultants, failure in anticipating the implications of the recommendations, inability to understand the poles of organisational politics of the client's organisation and communication gaps with the clients people due to ego problems. Therefore these problems need to be tackled to improve the quality of service.

(iv) With regard to the status of consultancy profession in India, literature survey reveals that most of the consultants are located in metros, state capitals and other important cities. Manufacturing is the main user, project consultancy, marketing and corporate strategy being main areas of consultation. The annual turnover of this sector was Rs. 2500 millions during 1993-94, average turnover being less than Rs. 3.5 lakhs. Hardly any direct marketing (3%) is being resorted to by this profession. Proper diagnosis of problems was reported to be done in lesser number of the cases. Consultant's man days is the most popular basis for charging consultancy fee, assignment basis being the dominant mode of engaging consultants. Majority of the consultants have experience of less than 10 years.

(v) On the basis of the review of articles of 25 practicing consultants serving SSIs conducted by the researcher, following conclusions can be drawn about the profile of management consultancy for SSIs.

(a) Consultancy needs of SSIs are integrated and undifferentiated in nature and vary at various stages. Unborn units/entrepreneurs/promoters require techno-economic and industrial consultancy. Pre-operative needs are entrepreneurial training and guidance with regard to various systems and procedures and formulation of corporate and functional strategies. Post-operation (normal) needs are with regards to review of systems and procedures and implementing desired change in various functional areas of management to solve various problems. Post-operation (expansion) needs are again techno-managerial in nature whereas post-operation (sick stage) needs are pertaining to detailed diagnostic study and formulation of techno-economic-cum-managerial package. Thus, technical, industrial and management consultancy services are required in form of a package for small scale unit which is not so in case of big unit which require specialised services.

(b) At present SSIs are mostly availing the services of consultants for feasibility/project reports, rehabilitation studies in case of sickness mostly to avail financial and other assistance/benefits from the financial institutions, industrial development agencies and govt. departments. Thus, at present the whole emphasis is on financial/other inputs and not on managerial inputs. Some stray cases of availing consultancy services for market survey productivity/profitability studies and modernisation studies have also been noticed.

(c) Use of consultancy during project implementation and post-production period is very low due to failure of entrepreneur to identify root cause of unsatisfactory performance on account of his incompetence and lack of proper records, reluctance to admit his own deficiencies and resultant tendency to blame external factors for all his failures, mistrust in the consultant and hesitation in providing real cost and profit data due to fear of misuse by the consultants, absence of suitable consultants in rural and semi urban areas, general shortage of good quality (also suitable) consultants, lack of training to entrepreneurs to enable them to identify their real problems, select a suitable consultant and going for management inputs in place of financial inputs as recommended by the consultant to solve the problems, lack of training to consultants for effective consultancy to small units, lack of data base on management consultants for the benefit of small scale sector and on consultancy needs of this sector for the benefit of consultants, viability problems of highly specialised private consultancy firms due to poor payment capacity of small units and elementary level of their needs.

(d) The suggestions given the authors to improve the quality of consultancy services for SSI units and utilisation can be summerised as under.

(1) Self dependent solo consultants with family support should be developed who could control and

supervise bare foot consultants for cheaper and simple consultancy services to small units.

(2) Training to all the consultants desirous of serving small units, about special features of small industry business management, methods of identifying their real problems (tools of financial analysis) and strategy for providing quality services with more emphasis on optimal use of existing resources than going for additional funds.

(3) Training to the entrepreneurs to enable them to see their problems in right perspective, make them aware about utility of management consultancy and methods to select and utilise consultants optimally, as apart of entrepreneurial development programs being run by various agencies.

(4) Planning commission should establish a management consultancy cell which should develop data on demand and supply of the management consultancy services by commissioning special studies from time to time.

(5) Consultants have to deal with small entrepreneurs very carefully due to ego problem, should go for long term relationship in form of retainer service and give simple suggestions with no emphasis on written reports. They could be asked to resolve the conflicts in partners, family members by clear allocation of duties etc.

(6) The financial institutions should establish a monitoring cell to identify problematic units early on the basis of feed back reports and ask them to hire a consultant of their choice to solve the problems, rather than wait till the unit becomes sick. This may be indicated in the terms and conditions of the loan agreement. If the unit refuses to do so then the FI may commence recovery proceedings.

(7) Quality of consultancy service could be measured on the basis of results of their recommendations.\

(8) The state directorate of industries should coordinate the activities of all the consultants serving the SSI sector with the help of the DICs and should solve their day to day problems.

(9) Strict code of conduct should be enforced by the govt. or some other professional body to ensure good quality consultation by the consultants.

(vi) Management consultancy services for SSI units in India is still its embryonic stage and is dominated by TCOs, SISI and NPC in the public/government/autonomous sectors followed by private consultants. DICs hardly provide any worthwhile consultancy services to SSI sector. However project/industrial consultancy is the major area of consultation to SSI in India and post production management consultancy is almost negligible even when majority of SSIs are not performing well.

(vii) It has been also reported that majority of even those SSI units who are not working satisfactorily are not utilising the services of the management consultants during the post production period.

On the basis of the inference drawn from the literature survey as summerised above, the research problem, objectives of research, research methodology etc. were specified and have been presented in this chapter in the subsequent sections.

1.1.3 Needs for this study

It is seen from the literature survey that on one hand majority of the SSI Units are not doing well mostly due the entrepreneurial and managerial inadequacies but on the other hand majority of the management consultants are not serving SSI units even when they are facing problems of viability. There may be several reasons for this paradox, the quality of consultancy services probably may be the prime reason.

Therefore there is need for study of quality dimensions of management consultancy services in detail to ascertain/ reconfirm the deficiencies in quality of services and other reasons for low utilisation of management consultancy services by SSI units during post production period revealed from literature survey for suggesting remedial measures. Hence this study.

1.2 THE RESEARCH PROBLEM

Taking into account the current status of knowledge in the area of management consultancy services for small scale industrial units in India, the research problem for this study has been specified to be the appraisal of the quality dimensions of the management consultancy services available for Small Scale Enterprises in India.

1.3 SIGNIFICANCE OF THE PROBLEM

The importance and various problems of SSI sector and the status of management consultants has already been reviewed above and it is seen that small scale units do not utilise the services of management consultants during post production period even when doing badly and management consultants find it difficult to survive. It has also been established by earlier researches that mis-management is major problem. Therefore the reasons underlying such state of affairs are required to be investigated. It is evident from the literature survey that finance is the major area in which small units require consultancy in the beginning itself followed by marketing and production. Therefore it will be worthwhile to appraise the utility of management consultancy services to small scale industries with regard to its quality keeping in view the perception of the SSI entrepreneurs. As the quality of services is closely associated with the cost of service, the viability of the consultancy firms is also to be examined and a workable model is to be suggested keeping in view the payment capacity of the small units and the viability requirement of the consultants. If this research is able to identify the real causes of the present states of affairs and is able to suggest remedial actions, it is expected to be very useful to the user small units, management consultants, policy makers, financial/developmental institutions including banks of not only India but other developing countries having similar socio- economical profile. The suggestions put forward by the author if implemented by the concerned institutions, may activate the latent demand for the management consultancy services from the SSI sector and consequently lead to healthy growth of consultancy sector. This will lead to better utilisation of vast financial resources blocked in this sector as well as growth in the employment in both the sectors leading to all round prosperity of the country. This research therefore, is considered to be very significant for not only India but other developing countries also.

1.4 OBJECTIVES OF THE STUDY

The main objective of this study is to appraise the quality of the management consultancy services available to SSI units in India but the specific objectives are as under.

(a) Identifying various aspects of existing management consultancy services such as types of services being offered, methods of charging consultancy fee, mode of engagement, organisational structure, types of organisations, employment profiles of consultants, background of consultants and the problems being faced by the consultants etc.

(b) Identifying various aspects of small scale industrial units such as level of performance, employment of management degree holders, management problems, problems while availing consultancy services, specific areas of management in which consultancy is required, reasons for lower utilisation of management consultancy services by SSI units, preferences for various consultancy practices, special features of consultancy services availed in the past (including level of satisfaction and relative importance of major causes of dissatisfaction), relative causes of low utilisation of consultancy services by SSI units and the remedial measures suggested by the users.

(c) Ascertaining the perception of third group i.e. financial institutions including banks etc. on various issues, of this study and compare with the perceptions of user group(SSI units and their associations) and the supplier group(management consultants and their association).

(d) Comparing and highlighting the gaps in the perception of supplier and user groups in reference to the perception of the third group i.e. FIs with regard to the management problems of SSI units, their real management consultancy needs, problems of the consultants and the users with each other, relative importance of management problems of SSI units, quality of services, choice of consultancy practices with regard to engagement and fee etc., causes of dissatisfaction of users, reason of low utilisation of management consultancy services by SSI units and suggestions to improve the present state of affairs.

(e) Identifying qualitative gaps in demand and supply of consultancy services for SSI units and also desired policies and practices.

(f) Suggesting ways to improve the quality of services and its use by the SSI units, reduce the cost of service keeping in view the payment capacity of SSI units and viability requirement of management consultants.

(g) Suggesting viable organisational model and policies for management consultants who wish to serve the SSI sector.

(h) Suggesting other remedial measures to be taken by SSI units, management consultants, their associations, developmental agencies, financial institutions and policy makers to facilitate optimal use of management consultancy services by the small scale sector.

(i) Suggesting future course of research in this area.

1.5 RESEARCH PROCEDURE

1.5.1 Nature of the problem

The problem under investigation is of ex-facto type, in which facts are already available and researcher has to just survey them, establish their present status and analyse the possible relationships amongst various variables of interest so as to validate the findings of the studies already done as well as identify new dimensions of the problem under study and highlight areas for further research.

1.5.2 Variables of interest

The variables of interest in this study are related to quality dimensions of management consultancy services available to small scale industries i.e. personal qualities of consultants, nature and policies of consultancy organisations, cost of service, the competence and commitment of the client, nature of consultant-client relationships, organisational climate of the client's firm and overall environmental factors. The related variables of interest are real management problems, consultancy needs of SSI sector, gap in demand and supply of various types of consultancy services as required by this sector, relative importance of various consultancy needs, causes of low utilisation of consultancy services by the small units and problems of both consultants and clients and suggestions to improve the current position.

1.5.3 The Research Design

As already discussed, this research is of descriptive nature of ex-facto type. Attempt has been made to answer the research questions related to the aims of this study with regards to the utility of management consultancy services available to the small scale industrial units. Research design of a problem under investigation is similar to a blue print of a building. It indicates the requirement of completing the research. The problems, the data and the inference are three area of activity involving research procedure.

The present investigation was divided into three phases. The first phase was planning phase which consisted of choosing general area of research, conducting literature survey to know as what has already been done, problem distillation taking into account the results of previous researches, objective specification, selection and construction of required tools, selection of sample including pre-sampling survey and preparation for collection of data. The second phase was execution phase which consisted of collection of data both through mail and field surveys from the selected respondents, screening the responses, tabulation of data as per pre-determined plan of analysis, application of suitable statistical tools for analysing data. The third phase was interpretation of the results of analysis, drawing inferences, answer the research questions and offer suitable suggestions including the areas for future research. The various activities of these phases may be shown as under:

Phase I- Planning phase

(1) Selection of a general problem area.

(2) Distillation of problem after reviews of related literature and detection of perception gaps.

(3) Specification of research objectives.

(4) Select suitable research design.

(5) Construction of appropriate tools depending upon research questions and designs.

(6) Selection of population and sample including pre-

sampling survey to identify the target population or subject pool.

(7) Preliminary preparation and time scheduling of field study.

Phase II- Execution phase

(1) Collection of data

(a) Administering the tools.

(b) Scoring the answer script.

(2) Treatment of data

(a) Tabulation of data.

(b) Statistical Analysis.

Phase III- Interpretation, inference and recommendations

(1) Interpret the results of statistical analysis.

(2) Answer the research questions.

(3) Suggest remedial measures.

(4) Suggest future areas of research.

1.5.4 Description of data gathering instruments

The present investigation required following types of questionnaires for collecting relevant data :-

(1) Questionnaire for management consultants to be administered on census basis to identify the target population of industrial units and the issues to be investigated with reference to the quality of management consultancy services. Questionnaires for management consultants were dispatched to all the consultants whose names and addresses could be collected through various sources. Besides other structural data, like constitution of the firm, annual turnover, pattern of employment, qualifications and experience of promoters and consultants, types of consultancy services being offered, method of charging consultancy fee, mode

of engagement, they were asked to indicate whether they serve small scale sector or not. If yes, then they were requested to indicate name and addresses of five SSI units which they have served in the past. If they did not serve SSI units then they were asked to indicate the reasons for not serving SSI units. Further they were asked to indicate the problems being faced while dealing with the SSI units, their perception about usefulness of this study and their suggestions to make this study more useful. This information was found to be very useful in drawing inferences about the structure of existing management consultancy services, framing questionnaire for the SSI units and also while interviewing the third parties. However most of the consultants were not ready to disclose the names of their clients.

(2) Detailed questionnaire for SSIs to know their status, background of the entrepreneurs, employment of management graduates,, satisfaction with current level of performance, perception of the entrepreneurs about utility of good management practices in solving management problems of SSIs, major management problems, major management consultancy needs, use of consultancy services, reasons for not using consultants/management consultants, feed back about the problem faced by them in selecting and utilising consultants in the past and their satisfaction with the quality of service, perception of the entrepreneurs about utility of management consultants in improving the efficiency of SSI units, their payment capacity, preference for mode of engagement, reasons for not using management consultants in post production period and their suggestions to improve the utility of management consultancy services for SSI sector.

(3) The opinion of the trade associations and FIs has been collected through unstructured interviews centering around the major management problems of SSI units, their management consultancy needs, reasons for not using consultancy services in post production period, their perception about quality of service and suggestions for improving the quality of services and utilisation of these services by SSI units.

The specimen questionnaires for the management consultants and the SSI units are placed at appendix B and C respectively.

1.5.5 Strategy adopted to improve the reliability and utility of the study

Following precautions were taken to improve the reliability of the data and for improving the response.

(a) Draft questionnaires were sent to following five experts for their opinion and suggestions and necessary modifications were made as suggested by them.

(1) Prof. S.K. Singh the then professor Indian Institute of Management /Lucknow ((India) now self employed.

(2) Prof. K. Ramchandran Indian Institute of Management/ Ahmadabad (India).

(3) Prof. S. Raghavan Faculty Member Management Development Institute, Gurgoan (Harayana) India.

(4) Dr. Gopinath, Director Consultancy Development Center, New Delhi, India.

(5) Mr. A. K. Bhatanagar, Managing Director, U.P. Industrial Consultants Ltd., Kanpur, India.

(b) An introduction highlighting the importance and utility of this study was incorporated in both the questionnaires to improve the response.

(c) The length of both the questionnaire was kept to be very short i.e. 2 pages for the management consultants and 4 pages for the SSI units.

(d) The questions have been kept as short and clear as possible.

(e) A self addressed and stamped envelop was enclosed with all the questionnaires to relieve the respondents (management consultants) from the burden of locating envelop, writing address and then stamping it.

TABLE 1.1

Objectives of this study

S.No.	*Objectives*	%
1	To identify real management needs of SSIs	42.00
2	To suggest ways to improve the awareness of the SSIs about importance of management consultancy services and remove negative perceptions on this account	20.00
3	To suggest solutions to the problems of under utilisation of management consultancy services by the SSIs	10.00
4	To identify problems of consultants while dealing with the SSIs	06.50
5	To suggest ways to reduce cost of consultancy services so as to bring it within the payment capacity of the SSIs	06.50
6	To comment upon quality aspects	03.00
7	To suggest viability models for the consultants who wish to serve small scale sector	03.00
8	To identify the terms and conditions under which SSI units want to avail consultancy services	03.00
9	To standardise the system of charging fee	03.00
10	To suggest ways to develop long term perspectives in both, the consultants and the SSIs	03.00
	Total	100.00

(f) A separate post box was got allotted in favour of the researcher in order to minimise the chances of disturbance of the incoming mail.

(g) In order to improve the reliability and utility of this study, all the management consultancy firms (1300 in numbers) were asked to state as what should be objects of this study and what steps should be taken to improve the utility of this study? However out of 103 consultants who replied to these questions either through mail or personal interviews, only 14 respondents replied to this question. Their responses have been analysed and the position is indicated below.

As such while specifying the aims of this study above views have been incorporated to the extent possible. Also while discussing matters with the SSI entrepreneurs, special emphasis was placed on the above aspects as far as possible and suggestions have been offered on above aspects based on the response of various groups.

TABLE 1.2

Steps suggested by respondents for increasing the utility of this study

S.No.	*Steps Suggested*	%
1	Interview the SSI entrepreneurs at their places to know their views face to face through cross questions.	50.00
2	If 95 consultants are contacted either through mail or personally all real issues to be probed with the SSIs can be ascertained.	14.00
3	It may be useful to talk to the industry associations to know their perceptions on various issues under investigation.	14.00
4	Concentrate only on quality aspects	07.40
5	Select only few areas and put the finding to use.	07.30
6	Give more weight to the views of the SSI units than other category of respondents.	07.30

The management consultants were also asked to offer their suggestions to make this study more useful for all concerned. The suggestions of the management consultants for improving the utility of this study are in Table 1.2.

Keeping in view the above feed back, the researcher has collected views of 103 consultants (over 95) and personally contacted 51 SSI entrepreneurs at their work place. Also the associations of consultants and SSIs were contacted wherever feasible to improve the reliability of the inferences. While discussing various issues with the SSI entrepreneurs best affords was made to ascertain their frank views on the quality of service, cost, reasons for low use of consultancy services and their suggestions on various important aspects, keeping in view the time and resource constraints.

1.5.6 Source of data

a) The names and addresses of the management consultants was compiled from the following sources.

1) The telephone directories of all the major cities.
2) List of the members of the Institute of management consultants of India (IMCI).
3) List of management consultants appended to the report on Management Consultancy Capability in India published by the Deptt of Scientific and Industrial research (DSIR), New Delhi.
4) Directory of management consultants of Consultancy Development Center (CDC), New Delhi.

(b) The secondary data about the present status of management consultants and the small scale sector has been collected through literature research and the reference is available in the bibliography.

(c) The name and addresses of SSI units were picked up from the directory of SSI units maintained by National Small Scale Industries Corporation for their purchase scheme.

(d) The field data has been collected by administering the questionnaires through mail and personal interviews. Unstructured interviews have been also conducted to ascertain the views of the trade associations and financial institutions.

1.5.7 Method of gathering data

The secondary data was gathered from the survey of available literature and the primary data through first through mail survey for the management consultants followed by field survey through survey research method. The whole emphasis has been on in-depth personal interviews of all the SSI entrepreneurs, selected management consultants and other related third parties so as to validate the views of the main parties to this research.

1.5.8 Population

The population of this study consists of about 30 lakhs SSI units and about 15000 management consultants. However the target population of the consultants i.e. those who actually provide management consultancy services, was not known. Therefore consultants providing management consultancy services were picked from the responses of the census survey of the management consultants conducted through the mail survey. It was decided to have a sample of at least 100 management consultants and 50 SSI units. It is a known facts from the literature survey that the TCOs and the SISIs serve the SSI sector in a big way. Therefore their representation in the sample has been kept higher than their actual share in the total strength of the management consultants.

1.5.9 The Samples

Samples were needed for collecting factual information/ views of suppliers, users and third groups. This section examines the nature and suitability of these sample in reference to the objectives of this research.

(I) THE SUPPLIER GROUP-MANAGEMENT CONSULTANTS AND THEIR ASSOCIATION

The sample of management consultants side includes 103 management consultants and their association i.e. Institute of management consultants of India (IMCI) Mumbai. The nature of this sample and its suitability has been examined and reported below.

(i) The nature of the sample

(a) Geographical Spread

The locations of the respondent management consultants has been analysed and the position is as under.

TABLE 1.3

Location Analysis of respondents management consultants

S.No.	*Place*	*Number of respondents*
1	2	3
1.	Mumbai	23
2.	Banglore	11
3.	Chennai	09
4.	Ahamadabad	07
5.	Hyderabad	06
6.	New Delhi	06
7.	Calcutta	05
8.	Vadodara	05
9.	Coimbtore	05
10.	Poona	04
11.	Patna	04
12.	Cochin	04
13.	Lucknow	02
14.	Agra	01
15.	Bareilly	01
16.	Azamgarh	01

1	2	3
17.	Simla	01
18.	Trivendrum	01
19.	Bharatpur	01
20.	Gurgoan	01
21.	Cuttuck	01
22.	Jalna	01
23.	Tinsukhiya	01
24.	Begusarai	01
25.	Gorakhpur	01
	Total	103

It may be seen from the above that respondents from almost all parts of the country have given their opinion in this study and such the results are expected to be reliable and representative. The regional status of the respondents is as under.

TABLE 1.4

Regional Profile of Management consultants

S.No.	*Region*	*No. of Respondents*	*%*
1	Western	35	34
2	Southern	36	34
3	Eastern	14	14
4	Northern	13	13
5	Central	05	05
	Total	103	100

Respondents from all regions have been selected. However share of Southern and Western regions is larger than eastern and northern regions. This is due to the fact that comparatively larger number of consultants are available in Western and Southern parts of the country. Since there is only one association of management consultants in India located in Mumbai, it was contacted and its views on important aspects were ascertained. Its views have been give due consideration and suitably incorporated while forming final views about the perception of supplier side.

(b) Sector profile

The sector analysis indicates the following position.

TABLE 1.5

Sector analysis of Respondent Consultants

S.No.	*Sector*	*No. of Respondents*	*%*
(1)	Private	81	78
(2)	Public	09	09
(3)	Govt.	07	07
(4)	Autonomous	06	06
	Total	103	100

Majority of the respondents(78%) are from the private sector followed by the public sector(9%), govt. organisations (7%) and autonomous consultancy organisations (6%). In fact majority of the consultants (shown to be over 95% by earlier studies) are in the private sector followed by govt. sector (3.0%), autonomous sector (1.5%) and public sector (0.50%). Although the number of public sector, autonomous sector and govt. consultants is quite small in that order of priority but they play significant role in extending consultancy services to the small scale industrial sector, as such higher percentage of these firms has been included in the sample.

(c) Age of the firms

In order to know the pattern of establishment of the consultancy firms, all respondents were asked to state their year of establishment and all except one replied to this question. The data has been arranged in two periods pre independence and post independence and then in the post independence era at a interval of 10 years. The position is as under.

It may be seen that the respondents are from all the periods.

TABLE 1.6

Age Analysis of the Consultancy Firms

S.No.	*Period*	*No. of Respondents*	*%*
1	Before 1947	01	01
2	1947-1956	09	09
3	1957-1966	08	08
4	1967-1976	27	26
5	1977-1986	31	30
6	1987-1996	27	26
7	Not given	01	01
	Total	103	100

(d) Constitutional profile

The respondents were asked to indicate the constitution of their firms and their responses have been analysed and the position is placed below.

TABLE 1.7

Constitution of the Consultancy firms

S.No.	*Constitution*	*No. of Firms*	*%*
1	Sole proprietorship	47	46
2	Pvt. Ltd.	20	20
3	Partnership	10	10
4	Public Ltd.	09	09
5	Society Act	09	09
6	Govt. Depts.	06	06
	Total	101	100

It is seen from the above that 46% of the respondents are sole proprietorship concerns, followed by Pvt. Ltd.(20%), Partnerships(10%), Public Ltd. and Societies(9% each) and

Govt. Enterprises(6%). However the actual combined share of sole proprietorship, Pvt. Ltd. and Partnership firms has been reported to be 97.50%, remaining being only 2.50%. However public sector and Govt. consultants are serving SSI sector in a big way and very few private sector consultants (Whose share is 97.50%) are serving this sector. Therefore they have been given more weightage in comparison to their actual share so as to have a representative view of this sector which is relevant for SSI sector.

(e) Annual Consultancy turnover

All the respondents were asked to indicate their annual consultancy turnover. All except 16 consultants replied to this question. The result of analysis of 87 consultants is as under.

TABLE 1.8

ANNUAL CONSULTANCY TURNOVER

S.No.	*Annual Turnover (Rs in lakhs)*	*No. of firms*	*%*
1	Free Services	02	2.30
2	Below 1.00	02	2.30
3	1.00-2.00	06	7.00
4	2.00-5.00	27	31.05
5	5.00-10.00	09	10.35
6	10.00-20.00	15	17.25
7	20.00-50.00	10	11.50
8	50.00- 100.00	06	7.00
9	100.00-1000.00	10	11.25
10	Above 1000.00	00	00.00
	Total	87	100.00

It is seen from the above that about 43% of the respondent firms have annual consultancy turnover of Rs 5 lakhs or below, 28% between Rs 5 lakhs and Rs 20 lakhs and about 30% above 20 lakhs. In actual practice around 90% of the consultancy firms have annual consultancy fee turnover of less than 5 lakes however due to inclusion of the technical consultancy organisations (TCO), which are mostly serving SSI units, the share of bigger firms has increased.

(f) Academic background of promoter consultants

All the promoter consultants were requested to indicate their academic and professional background and their responses have been analysed. The analysis reveals the following position.

TABLE 1.9

Academic background of the promoter consultants

S.No.	*Academic Qualifications*	*No. of consultancy firms*	*%*
1	B.Tech./M.Tech.	42	42.90
2	Engg. with M.B.A.	12	12.25
3	M.B.A.	23	23.50
4	M.Com./M.A.(Econ.)	10	10.20
5	B.A./M.A.	02	2.00
6	F.C.A./I.C.W.A./C.S.	06	6.15
7	Any other	03	3.00
	Total	98	100.00

It is seen from the above analysis that about 55% of the respondent promoters have technical background out of which 12.25% have management degree. Similarly 35% of the respondents are having management degrees out of which 23% have pure management degree. Promoters with other professional degree are 10.20 % having commerce /economics degrees and 6% are chartered or cost accountants, while remaining 5% have other degrees. Thus, it appears that over 90% of the promoters are professionals. Therefore, why they are not able to provide quality consultancy services to SSIs is be investigated.

(g) Experience profiles of the promoter consultants

Apart from the academic qualifications, all the respondents were requested to indicate the duration of experience. The data about their experience have been analysed and the results are as under.

TABLE 1.10

Experience profiles of the promoter consultants

S.No.	*Duration experience (years)*	*No. of consultancy firms*	%
1	Below 5 years	00	00
2	5-10	01	01
3	10-15	05	05
4	15-20	20	20
5	Above 20 years	74	74
	Total	100	100

It is seen that 74% of the respondents have above 20 years of experience and another 20% have experience of between 15 to 20 years. Thus, over 94% have experience above 15 years, the experience can be prima facie considered suitable for quality consultancy services. Therefore, why they are not able to provide quality consultancy services to SSIs is to be probed in depth.

(ii) The suitability of the sample

It may be seen that the nature of the sample is urban based and relatively smaller in size in reference to the population size. However, taking into account the fact that IMCI, i.e. the only association of management consultants having around 300 members has been also included in the sample of the supplier group and their views taken on important aspects, the sample is considered suitable and may be able to throw sufficient light on the issues under study.

(II) THE USER GROUP- SMALL SCALE ENTERPRISE AND THEIR ASSOCIATIONS

(i) The nature of the sample

The author conducted in-depth interview of 51 SSI units and seven SSI associations to ascertain their views about various aspects of this study. This section examines the nature of the sample and see how it may be able to serve the limited purpose of this study. The following aspects of the sample of SSI units and their associations have been analysed and the results are presented below:

(a) Geographical spread

The location analysis reveals as under.

TABLE 1.11

Locations of respondent SSI units

S.No.	*Place*	*No. of SSI units*	*%*
1	Chennai	07	12
2	Vadodara	05	10
3	Ahmedabad	05	10
4	Hyderabad	05	10
5	Coimbatore	05	10
6	Bangalore	05	10
7	Trivendrum	03	06
8	Nagpur	03	06
9	Kota	02	04
10	NOIDA	02	04
11	Agra	02	04
12	Cochin	02	04
13	Hazipur	02	04
14	Azamgargh	01	02
15	Gorakhpur	01	02
16	Samastipur	01	02
	Total	51	100

It may be seen from the above that almost all parts of the country have been covered in this study to have representative views. Similarly Small Industry Associations located at Gorakhpur, Agra (both in northern India), Vadodara, Ahmadabad (both in the western India), Chennai, Bangalore and Coimbatore (all the three in Southern India) were also contacted and their views on important issues obtained through personal interview by the researcher. Therefore, the sample is geographically well spread.

(b) Age of the firms

All respondents were asked to indicate the year of establishment of their unit. The analysis of the age data indicates pattern indicated below.

TABLE 1.12

Year of establishment

S.No.	*Year*	*No. of SSI units*	*%*
1	Before 1947	02	3.90
2	1947-1956	00	0.00
3	1957-1966	01	1.96
4	1967-1976	13	25.49
5	1977-1986	20	39.22
6	1987-1996	15	29.41
	Total	51	100.00

It may be seen that most of the respondent units were established after 1967 (94%) and very few units were available prior to this period. However, most of the units are having operational age of over 5 years. This is sufficient for having realistic responses from the entrepreneurs.

(c) Constitutional profile

The constitution of the respondent units are as under.

The intention was to contact those entrepreneurs of SSI

units who may have professional background and are able to reply to the queries. As such more number of Private Ltd. and Public Ltd. units were selected. The subject of management consultancy being highly technical, this was felt essential. Here judgmental sampling technique was followed.

TABLE 1.13

Constitution of respondent SSI units

S.No.	*Constitution*	*No. of Units*	*%*
1	Sole proprietorship	12	23.53
2	Partnership	13	25.49
3	Pvt. Ltd.	22	43.14
4	Public Ltd.	04	7.84
	Total	51	100.00

(d) Investment profile

All the respondents were requested to indicate the investment made in their factory at original value. The data received from them has been analysed and the following pattern emerges.

TABLE 1.14

Investment pattern

S.No.	*Range of investment (Rs. in lakhs)*	*No. of firms*	*%*
1	Below 5.00	06	12.50
2	Above 5.00 but below15.00	10	21.00
3	Above 15.00 but below 25.00	06	12.50
4	Above 25.00 but below 50.00	15	31.50
5	Above 50.00 but below 100.00	06	12.50
6	Above100.00 but below 300.00	01	02.00
7	Small scale sector	04	08.00
	Total	48	100.00

It may be seen from the above that units from all the investment brackets have been picked up for the present investigation. However this is not for any generalisation about the actual investment pattern which is actually biased in favour of tiny and cottage units having investment below Rs 5.00 lakhs (about 90%).

(e) Capacity utilisation profile

The pattern of capacity utilisation of the respondent firms is as under.

TABLE 1.15

Pattern of capacity utilisation

S.No.	*Range of utilisation*	*No of SSI units*	*%*
1	Below 25%	02	4.20
2	Above 25%but below 50%	03	6.20
3	Above 50% but below 75%	25	52.10
4	Above 75%	14	29.20
6	Totally labour based	04	08.00
	Total	48	100.00

It may be seen from the above that over 60% of the units are having capacity utilisation below 75%. Though the respondent SSI units are relatively better placed, actually majority of the units do not perform well.

(f) Background of respondent entrepreneurs

The data with regard to the academic and the professional qualifications of the promoters of the respondents units has been analysed and the position is as in Table 1.15.

It will be seen from the above that over 70% of the respondents are professionals. Though the entrepreneurs of the small scale sectors are mostly under qualified, the researcher has deliberately chosen the relatively better qualified entrepreneurs just to ensure that they are in a position to understand the concepts of management consultancy and contribute effectively to this research.

TABLE 1.15

Academic and professional background of respondent entrepreneurs

S.No.	*Qualifications*	*No of units*	*%*
1	B.Tech/ M. Tech	27	52.94
2	Engg with M.B.A.	02	03.92
3	M.B.A.	03	05.89
4	M.Com./ M.A.(Eco.)	04	07.84
5	B.A/M.A	13	25.49
6	Under graduates	02	03.92
	Total	51	100.00

(g) Experience profile of the respondents

The data related to experience of the entrepreneurs has been analysed and the position is as under.

TABLE 1.16

Experience Profiles of respondent entrepreneurs

S.No.	*Experience in years*	*No of units*	*%*
1	Below 5.00	05	10..00
2	>5.00<10.00	07	14.00
3	>10.00<15.00	05	10.00
4	>15.00<20.00	05	10.00
5	>20.00	28	56.00
	Total	50	100.00

It is seen that 76% of the entrepreneurs have experience of 10 years or above. This was deliberately done (judgmental sampling) to have respondents who could understand the issue under investigation and could offer useful suggestions.

It is further seen that 57% of the entrepreneurs have experience in the same line whereas remaining have experience in other areas.

(ii) The suitability of the sample

It may be seen that though the sample is urban based but given the complexity of the concept of management consultancy under study and the fact that views of seven SSI associations well spread over the country representing sizable number of SSIs also located in the semi-urban and rural areas, have been taken on important issues, it is considered suitable for the purpose of this study.

(III) THE EFFICACY OF THE SAMPLES FOR THE STUDY

In view of the justification given above about the samples of users and supplier groups and the fact that questionnaires were mailed to 1300 consultants but only 80 responses were received out of which only 65 were found to be relevant, in-depth nature of interviews conducted across the length and width of India by the researcher, excessive cost of field survey and the intensive interview of seven financial institutions to have a reference point for important issues, the samples are considered suitable for specific purpose of examining the quality dimensions of management consultancy services for SSI units in India.

1.5.10 Plan of analysis

Data collected has been analysed to know the following dimensions of this problem, keeping in view the objective of this study.

(a) The supplier Group- Management Consultants and Their Association

(1) Employment pattern of the consultants.

(2) Background of consultants.

(3) Types of consultancy services being offered and their relative importance.

(4) Method of charging consultancy fee.

(5) Mode of engagement.

(6) Whether serving SSI units.

(7) Share of SSI sector in the total turnover of consultancy firms serving SSI sector.

(8) Reasons for not serving Small units

(9) Major problems being faced by the consultants while serving SSI units and their relative importance.

(10) Steps suggested by the consultants to improve the utility of this study (for use during the survey of the SSI units).

(b) The User Group- Small Scale Industrial Units and Their Associations

1. Employment pattern of the management graduates/ diploma holders.
2. Level of satisfaction with the present level of performance.
3. Perception of the respondents about the utility of good management practices in solving the internal problems and minimising the adverse impact of external problems.
4. Major management problems and their relative importance.
5. Major management consultancy needs and their relative importance.
6. Extent of utilisation of the services of management consultant in the past.
7. Major reasons for not using management consultancy services and their relative importance.
8. Perception of the respondents about usefulness of management consultants in improving the efficiency of the SSI units.

9. The payment capacity of the respondents.
10. Desired mode of engagement of the consultants preference of the respondents.
11. Reasons for not availing services of the management consultants in solving post production problems even when they exist and their relative importance.
12. Major suggestions of the respondents to solve the present paradox and for improving the quality of the existing management consultancy services and their relative importance.

Experience of the SSI units with regards to use of consultants in the past are planned to be analised on lines indicated below.

1. Type of consultant used (private/public sector/ govt./Autonomous).
2. Nature of assignment.
3. Fee paid.
4. Basis of charging fee.
5. Time taken in completing the assignment.
6. Status of implementation of the recommendations.
7. Level of satisfaction (in %).
8. Methods adopted to identify the problems.
9. Method followed to select the particular consultant.
10. Whether the original expectations communicated clearly to the consultant in advance?
11. Status of consultancy contract.
12. Clarity of terms and conditions.
13. Major deficiencies noticed and their relative importance.
14. Benefits accrued to the respondent units in reference to the fee paid.
15. Major problems encountered while availing the consultancy services.

16. Whether the same consultant will be repeated? (yes/no)

(c) The Responses of the Third Group i.e. Financial Institutions

(1) Major internal management problems of the small scale sector and their relative importance.

(2) Major management consultancy needs of the SSI units.

(3) Major reasons for not using the services of the management consultants in the post production period even when they are not doing well and their relative importance.

(4) Major recommendations to improve the utilisation of the management consultancy services to solve post production problems by the SSI units and their relative importance.

(5) Their recommendations about other aspects.

(e) Comparison of the views/perceptions of the supplier group i.e. management consultants and IMCI on one hand and the user group i.e. SSI entrepreneurs and their associations on the other and the financial institutions on following dimensions of consultation process so as to identify the perception gaps and its ramifications.

1. Relative importance of various internal management problems of SSI units.
2. Relative importance of the real management consultancy needs of the SSI units.
3. The management problems of the SSI units vis-à-vis their real consultancy needs.
4. The actual demand of management consultancy services by SSI units (actual consultancy needs) vis-à-vis supply of such serves (the consultancy services being made available by the management consultants).

5. Actual management consultancy needs of SSIs vis-à-vis the consultancy services actually availed by them.
6. The reasons for not utilising the management consultancy services by the SSI units and their relative importance.
7. The relative importance of major reasons for lower utilisation of consultancy services by the SSI units vis-à-vis major reasons for not serving the SSI sector as reported by consultants.
8. The relative importance of the major problems of the consultants while dealing with the SSI units vis-à-vis major problems of the SSI units while dealing with the consultants.
9. Methods of charging consultancy fee by the consultants vis -a-vis methods employed by the user SSI units to pay the consultancy fee in the past.
10. Mode of engagement reported by the consultants vis-à-vis mode of engagement desired by the SSI units.
11. Extent of use of consultants by the SSI units vis-à-vis extent of service to the SSI units by the consultants.
12. Sector of the Consultants available vis-à-vis sector of the consultants used by the SSI respondents.
13. The usefulness of the management consultants in improving the performance of the SSI units.
14. The suggestions to improve the utilisation of management consultancy services by the SSI units and their relative importance.
15. Relative importance of the suggestions given to improve the quality of consultancy services to SSI sector.
16. Relative importance of various suggestions for a viable marketing strategy.

17. Relative importance of suggestions to reduce the cost of consultancy services to the SSI sector.

1.5.11 Statistical tools used for analysis

The statistical tools used are very simple and of following types.

1. Tally marking method to tabulate the responses of various category of respondents.
2. Percentages of various attributes in reference to the total tally marks.
3. Simple additions to have total number of consultants having different academic backgrounds as well as experience profiles.

1.6 Scope of the study

As already stated in the objectives, the primary aim of this study is to appraise the quality dimensions of management consultancy service, it was planned to conduct in-depth discussions with the selected SSI entrepreneurs on various related issues after collecting data about their units. The subject matter of this study being quality of management consultancy services, only a person of reasonably high academic background and long experience, with progressive outlook, who has either dealt with management consultants in the past or possess high level of general awareness about them, could contribute fruitfully to the discussions. Therefore, it was decided to interact with at least 50 entrepreneurs operating in major cities in various industrial estates, where management consultants are also available. As such it has not been possible to contact SSI units located in rural areas. Similarly responses of 103 management consultants has been analysed. Secondly the study concentrates on quality dimensions only though data about quantitative aspects of management consultants as well as SSI units has been collected to the extent possible just to evaluate the effectiveness of the samples.

1.7 Limitations of the study

No research study is without limitations and the findings are to be appreciated in the context of such limitations. This study is also subject to following limitations.

(a) As a matter of policy, the perception of the user groups i.e. SSI units and their associations, has been given more weightage over the perceptions of the other categories of respondents on the basic principle that the customer is the final decider. Also due care has been taken in selecting the respondents with regard to their level of awareness. However it is quite possible that some of SSI respondents may not have complete knowledge of this area or might have even tried to conceal their own shortcomings and might have blamed consultants or/and other external agencies for their own failures. This imperfection may have adverse impact on the quality of inferences drawn.

(b) The sample of respondents SSI entrepreneurs is restricted to 51 units out of the total population of 30 lakhs SSI units and that too in few big cities. However this became inevitable to control the cost of the study and to get competent respondents for in-depth interviews as discussed in the scope of this study. However to make good any deficiency on this account, the views of seven industry associations has been also collected through personal interviews and this is expected to balance the views of the SSI users.

(c) Initially questionnaires were sent to 1300 management consultants whose names and addresses could be collected from all possible sources and all precautions were taken to increase the responses but only 80 consultants replied out of which only 65 were found to be relevant. In order to make good this deficit, another 38 management consultants were contacted during the field study. Therefore the sample is based on field response and only includes management consultants interested in this study (convenience sampling).

(d) The possible lack of appreciation of the problem in all its dimensions by various respondents may affect the quality of results but best efforts have been made to contact only the promoters having sufficient experience and calibre.

(e) The sample of management consultants is skewed towards bigger govt/semi-govt. organisations due to inclusion of TCOs. This was done to give adequate representation to them who primarily serve the SSI sector.

(f) The owners of the SSI units being very busy persons could not devote more than 30 minutes to the researcher. Therefore the aspects which could be discussed with them were restricted to the most essentials ones. As such all attention was concentrated to discuss the issue of quality of service in reference to their management problems, low use of management consultancy services by them and what could be done to improve the situation.

(h) The researcher himself being a management consultant for about 7 years with one of the TCOs could influence the fairness of the study by bringing in, his own bias or pre-conceived ideas. However best efforts have been made to base the inferences only on the data and opinions obtained from literature/mail/field surveys.

Therefore this present study with all its limitations stated above is expected to throw sufficient light on the issues involved and may tend to be stepping stone for further research in this area.

1.8 Operational definitions of various concepts used in this study

In order to have full understanding of the correct scope of this research, it is essential to establish the operational definitions of various terms i.e. consultation, management consultancy and small scale industrial unit.

(a) Consultation

Ronald Lippit (132) has defined consultation as under,

> "Consultation relationship is a voluntary relationship between professional helper (consultant) and help seeking system (client) in which consultant is attempting to help the client in solving some current or potential problem(s) and the relation is perceived to be temporary by both the parties. Also consultant is an outsider."

Taking into account the functional view of consultancy, Fritz Steel has defined consultation process as under:

> "By consultation process I mean any form of providing help on the contents, process, or structure of a task, where the consultant is not actually responsible for doing the job himself but helping those who are."

Thus consultation is temporary help by an outside helper to solve any problem without any compulsion. Author has accepted this definition with the alteration that consultant can also be appointed on the intervention of third parties such as creditors etc. and in such a situation the relationship does not remain voluntary. Secondly according to Lippit, consultant is an outsider. It is seen that in many cases, larger organisations have internal consultancy divisions to advise their line staff like consultancy cells of commercial banks and few business houses. Fritz Steel has therefore not included the concept of outsider in his definition. The researcher also agrees with Lippit and as such has excluded in house consultancy services available only to the parent organisation. Lippit has also perceived the relationship to be temporary. However the researcher has included the concept of retainership which may be relatively longer relationship but is essentially temporary.

(b) Management Consultancy.

Management consultancy for the operational entrepreneur implies a planned process to modify attitudes, increase knowledge, improve/ develop systems and skills through learning experience to achieve better performance in one or range of activities to meet current or / and future requirement of our organisation. It aims at sustained growth of organisation by making the entrepreneur more growth oriented, flexible, innovative and adoptive. Thus management consultancy is a very wide field and could include any body who gives significant advice for better management starting from the suppliers and agents to pure management consultants.

However the concept of management consultancy has been defined by various authors/organisations as under.

(1) The institute of management consultants of U.K. defines management consultancy as under.

"Services provided by an independent and qualified person or persons in identifying and investigating problems concerning policy, organisation, procedures and methods, recommending appropriate actions and helping to implement these recommendations."

(2) According to ILO book on " Management consultancy - A guide to the profession.:" by M. Kubr (120), management consultancy is

" An independent advisory service providing professional knowledge and skills relevant to practical management problems."

(3) According to Green and Mefzer, management consultancy is

" Service provided by specially trained and qualified person who assists in an objective and independent manner, the organisations (clients) to identify management problems and help them when required, in implementation of solutions."

Thus it is evident from the above 3 sets of definitions of management consultancy that it is independent and objective service thus excludes internal service, is advisory and most important it helps in solving management problems to enhance overall organisational effectiveness of the client. Now it is to be decided as what are management problems. Here the institute of management consultants defines these to be problems concerning policy, organisation and systems/ procedures. As already discussed earlier the consultancy needs of small scale units can not be divided into technical and managerial and they mostly require technical, economic, legal and managerial services in one package. It is further noticed that most of their post- operational problems have their roots in pre-production blunders connected to project and financial decisions. Therefore they require integrated services without any high degree of technical or managerial expertise. Therefore taking into account the field reality services required to solve problems related to project decisions, project implementation, operations and expansion of a unit have been included in management consultancy services. However the consultants who do not have expertise in the areas of management such as organisation, policy, procedure/systems have been termed as industrial consultants and not as management consultants. Pure management consultants who do not have any expertise in the area of project identification, market surveys, project/ feasibility reports and project implementation etc. including liaison with the financial institutions and developmental agencies, are hardly of any use to a small scale unit. At the same time an industrial consultant not having any managerial expertise will also leave these units high and dry after they commence commercial production and it is quite likely that unit may become sick due to faulty post-production policies, procedures and organisation etc. Therefore industrial/project consultancy has been included in management consultancy services for the purpose of this research.

(c) Small Scale Industrial Units (SSIs)

According to the current definition of govt of India (1990), an industrial unit having investment in plant and machinery below Rs 60 lakhs is termed as small scale unit. Unit which invests Rs 5 lakhs or below in plant and machinery, is classified as tiny unit, but such unit totally based on household is termed as cottage unit.

It has been mentioned earlier that small units are normally not able to employ persons having managerial capability on full time basis due to financial constraints and as such require external help. However units having an investment of Rs 50 lakhs or more in fixed assets may be quite capable of engaging management degree holders on full time basis. Therefore the researcher has deliberately considered all units including tiny as well as cottage units as Small Scale unit in variation to the technical definition of the government of India for the purpose of this study. However only industrial units have been included in the this definition by the researcher.

Thus the context of consultation, management consultancy and SSI units should be very clear to the readers in the context of this study.

1.9 The layout of the book

This book aims at presenting the findings of research study to appraise the quality of management consultancy services available to Small Scale Industrial Units in India for the benefits of the academic fraternity and future researchers so as to facilitate further research in this area. The book has been devided into seven chapters. The first chapter presents the background of the research endeavor based on the research/studies already done including research methodology. The survey of literature on the works already done has been presented in the second chapter. Third, fourth and fifth, chapters present the analysis of the facts and perceptions of the supplier, user and third groups on various aspects of the quality of management consultancy services available to SSI units in India. The sixth chapter analises and compares the perception of various respondents groups about relevant aspects, brings out the gaps and then concludes. Finally the seventh chapter presents the conclusions and then inferences drawn by the author on the basis of results of analysis of the field data in reference to the findings of the literature research and his recommendations for improving the quality of management consultancy services and also its utilisation by the Small Scale Industrial Units for benefit of consultancy profession, small scale sector and agencies involved in financing and development of these sectors. The bibliography, questionnaires for management consultants, SSI units and references for further readings are placed at appendix A to E respectively.

2

Literature Survey

This study aims at appraisal of the quality of management consultancy services available to SSI units in India. In order to ascertain various dimensions of this activity including current status of knowledge, survey of related literature was conducted by the researcher and the results are reported in this chapter. The results of literature survey about the user group (SSI units) and the supplier group (management consultants) can be summerised as under.

2.1 THE CUSTOMERS GROUP— SMALL SCALE ENTERPRISES AND THEIR ASSOCIATIONS

2.1.1 The Problems of Industrial Sector in general

Review of related literature, reveals that there are about 3 millions SSI units in India employing about 15 millions persons and they constitutes about 95% of the total number of industrial units available in the country. It is further seen that the performance of industrial sector has been quite unsatisfactory. Several studies have been conducted to identify the problems (causes) responsible for this state of affairs. However only few of them have been reviewed by the researcher in order to have a general idea about the major problems.

(i) S.N. Bidani and P.K. Mishra (23) have analysed the anatomy of industrial sickness and have concluded that mis-management leads to following secondary internal problems in various functional areas leading to increased cost of products/services.

(a) *Finance:* Inappropriate financial structure, inefficient inventory management, absence of proper costing and cost control system, lack of financial planning and controls leads to lower productivity of capital and higher financial charges.

(b) *Production:* Selection of wrong machines, capacity bottlenecks, unsuitable site, inadequate material controls, faulty maintenance, improper quality controls and slow product development due to inadequate R&D leads to low capacity utilisation and increase in cost due to higher absorption of overhead costs. Similarly low quality leads to higher rejections and loss of market.

(c) *Marketing:* Inaccurate demand projection at the project formulation stage leads to selection of wrong project and capacity. Similarly inappropriate product mix, lack of product up-gradation coupled with weak sales promotion affects the sales adversely. Lastly dependence on only few customers makes the demand very risky. All these failures lead to lower sales and lower profitability.

(d) *Personnel:* Absence of manpower planning, ad hoc salary and incentive system, inadequate grievance handling system leads to all round frustration in the employees resulting into poor manpower productivity. This leads to increased labour cost per unit of production.

(e) *Corporate Management:* Ad hocism due to vague corporate mission and objectives, lack of inter-departmental coordination, conflicts/disputes in the owners/partners and low adaptability to environmental changes leads to wastage of resources of the organisation i.e. man, money, machines and materials.

Besides above internal problems, industrial units face a number of external problems in various functional areas. These may be credit constraints, delays in sanctions and disbursement of loans, all round corruption in financial institutions and government agencies, shortage of quality materials, fast changing technology, lack of competent technical personnel in the nearby areas, unplanned licensing by the govt., lack of reliable data base, frequent changes in fiscal policies of govt., market recession, inter union rivalry including political effluence and crime syndicates etc. All these factors are related to the environment in which the unit is functioning and could be tackled up to some extant by frequent SWOT analysis and taking required corrective/adaptive steps. Management is not totally helpless in these areas also.

(ii) A study by the Reserve Bank of India on industrial sickness haas also concluded that 52% of the units were sick due to mis-management followed by marketing problems.

(iii) Sharu S. Rangnakar (182) analyses the causes of industrial sickness and concludes that it is managerial sickness that can be cured. Environmental sickness forces unit to change its course of business. Similarly nothing can be done in case of entrepreneurial sickness which is due to lack of integrity on the part of entrepreneur. However the commitment of the managers makes all the difference. According to him, sick managers can be of three types i.e Bandwallas-those who look very busy but hardly deliver any results; child widows-those who are themselves frustrated and frustrate others by spreading pessimism and Pindaris-those who are totally corrupt and suck the blood of the organisation through commissions etc. Bandwallas and child widows could be controlled by tight monitoring and controls but the Pindaries are to be eliminated or cornered to a dry post. Rangnekar stresses that unless the quality of managers is improved, any amount of structural changes and infusion of additional capital is not going to help. Commitment and integrity are most important elements of success. This is felt necessary to solve the secondary internal and external problems identified by Bidani and Mishra (23).

(iv) P.K.Yadav and Rajkamal (240) have conducted in-depth study of an industrial unit and conclude that mis-management coupled with heavy overheads and marketing are major problems. However heavy overheads and marketing are result of faulty business strategy, which again is a managerial function.

On the basis of four sample studies quoted above, it can be concluded that major challenge before the industrial sector today is mis-management, which could be deliberate or due to lack of competency. It is in the second area that an unit can be helped by any external agency and hardly any help is possible when the promoters/management lack integrity and commitment.

2.1.2 Problems of Small Scale Sector

(I) The management problems of SSIs

Numerous researches/studies have been conducted on the problems of small scale sectors including sickness in this sector. A few of them have been selected for review to identify major problems and their relative roles in the sickness/bad performance of this sector.

(i) Vidya Sager Gupta (79) has identified the following problems which are internal to the SSI units.

(a) *Pre-production problems:* These include planning mistakes such as selection of wrong project/product idea, project size, site and plant due to incorrect assessment of demand and customer's choice due to lack of proper data base, avoidable higher investment in non-productive fixed assets, wrong project appraisal by financial institutions and banks due to corruption and/or lack of expertise and acceptance of such projects by them, delays in obtaining various facilities such as sanctions and disbursement of loan and lack of coordination in promoters or partners and various agencies.

(b) Post-production problems: These are poor maintenance, lack of material controls and bad quality, in the area of the production; lack of market research, faulty marketing and sales strategy and lack of product development in the area of marketing; uneconomical purchases, lack of supplier's credit, avoidable increase in inventory in the area of material management, inefficient management of working capital, absence of costing and cost control systems, unplanned payments and diversion of funds in the area of finance and bad labour-management; relations in the area of personnel management. All of the above lead to low capacity utilisation and resultant increase in the cost of production.

(ii) Renu Singh Parmar (165) also discusses the problems but at different stages such as conception of the project idea, project planning and implementation under pre-production stage and various operational and managerial problems during post implementation stage. It is said that internal problems are related to management dyfunctions and the external to the environmental factors. The impact of external factors can also be minimised by suitable management of pre-production lapses. Apart from what has been discussed by Vidya Sagar Gupta, She has added the unsuitable background of the entrepreneur and low level of commitment on his part as another major internal cause. She has also emphasised importance of technical competence during implementation phase along with inadequate mobilisation of funds by the promoters, frequent changes in site plans. Lack of expansionist market strategy and narrow market base has been added in the area of marketing.

(iii) P.K. Panda and R.K. Mehar (163) have studied 25 sick and 15 normal units of Jagatpur Industrial Area of Urrisa and have found that cost escalation was more prominent in case of sick units (47%) than healthy units (9%). Most of the sick units took 2 to 3 years in commencing production and became sick even before starting production. They have found that lack of techno- economic factors are dominated by marketing and investment bottlenecks. Lack of integrity has been noticed as major cause like reported by Renu Singh Parmar (165) as 30% to 40% of the entrepreneurs left their units in sick condition.

(iv) P.K. Mishra (150) has studied 30 sick and 30 healthy units of Adityanager Industrial Estate of Jamshedpur and has concluded that lack of entrepreneurship is the basic cause of sickness as it affects both internal and external factors.

(II) Relative importance of various management problems of SSIs

A number of studies leave been done to ascertain the relative importance of various problems. A few of them have been appraised below to have on overview

(a) Vidya Sager Gupta (79) rates finance as the main cause of sickness followed by lack of raw materials, bad quality of products, marketing and bad debt.

(b) Baldin Garge (69) also rates finance as main cause followed by marketing and production.

(c) G Srinivasan (212) also rates finance as main cause followed by production, lack of raw material and then mis-management.

(d) NASII and NAYE rate marketing as the main cause.

(e) M.C. Shetty (201) rates finance (lack of working capital) as the main cause.

(f) Usha Arora and R.R.Azad (9) also rate finance as no I problem.

(g) Ashok Shukla (202) rates finance (lack of working capital) as the prime cause followed by lack of raw materials.

(h) Manohar Dashpande (50) says that 73% of the units were working below their rated capacity due to low working capital followed by ad hoc marketing and lack of raw materials.

(i) S.V.S. Sharma (198) who has studied comparative problems of the developing Asian countries, also concludes that finance is main problem followed by labor troubles, marketing and management inadequacy.

(j) N.S. Toor (228) also indicates that SSI units are mostly tiny and finance is their major problem (35%) followed by marketing (14%), raw materials (10%), disputes in promoters (3.7%) and labour troubles (2.2%).

(k) Nayyar committee of RBI has also concluded that SSI units get only 8.1% of their annual turnover as working capital loan against desired level of 20%. The committee has further indicated that bigger SSI units corner larger loans (18%) at the cost of tiny units who hardly get 2.7% of their annual turnover as working capital loan.

It is evident from the above studies, which are mostly based on entrepreneur's perception, that financial constrain is major problem followed by either raw materials or marketing. In other words there is emphasis on the external factors. However there are studies which have accessed the perceptions of entrepreneurs in the light of opinions of others such as financial institutions, management consultants and other opinion leaders. Some of these studies have been appraised and findings are as under.

(a) Prithpal Singh (207) who studied the exogenous and endogenous causes of sickness, concludes that mismanagement is critical factor for small scale units due to razor thin viability.

(b) C.K.Mann, M.S.Grindle and P.Shipton (144) discuss the role of development agencies and say that they are impractical.

(c) Milton C. Lancenstien (128) says that SSIs are unable to manage expansion and require external help.

(d) Jani D.K. (102) concludes that marketing and escalation in project cost are two major problems.

(e) B.K.Dikxit (53) concludes that lack of managerial attributes in the entrepreneurs is main cause followed by production, marketing, and finance. He found that 70% of the units did not have any planning and non-agro units were facing more marketing problems. He blamed govt. for giving entry to incompetent entrepreneurs.

(f) B.N. Singh (204) blames tèchnical incompetence for all production and quality problems. Similarly K.S. Sriram (213) blames bad quality of materials for quality problem and rejections.

(g) Renu Singh Parmar (165) has studied impact of external vis-a vis internal problems and concludes that they have 59.2% and 40.8% share in the sickness respectively. Further while ranking internal problems, she concludes that management inadequacy is main cause (53.6%) followed by poor quality (12.8%), diversion of funds (12.5%), delay in implementation (10%) and labour troubles (10%). However ranking of external problems indicates that marketing is main problem (42%) followed by working capital problem (19.5%), adverse govt. policies (18.5%) and delays in implementation due to external problems (15%).

(h) P.K. Panda and R.K. Mehar (163) conclude that delay in implementation and resultant escalation in project cost is main cause.

(i) P.K.Mishra (150) concludes that lack of entrepreneurship leads all other internal factors.

(j) K.K.Sexena (193) also concludes that managerial inadequacy is major cause followed by faulty appraisal of the project by the financial institutions.

Above review therefore reveals that managerial inadequacy in the area of finance, project management and marketing coupled with technical incompetence is the major challenge before the SSI units.

2.1.3 Dimensions of entrepreneurial inadequacies

Review of literature on problems of industrial units has already revealed that lack of entrepreneurial, managerial and technical skills on the part of promoters is major cause of unsatisfactory performance of small scale sector. Most of the small units are one man show and are hardly in a position to employ any other employee with requisite expertise. Therefore, it has been considered worthwhile to review the literature pertaining to ideal entrepreneurial traits, existing profiles and major problems in this area.

(a) Ideal Entrepreneurial Traits

Researcher has reviewed the studies of Manfred F.R. Kete de Vris (143), Satish Taneja (220), Ian Duncan (54), Hosmer, Cooper and Vesper (90), M.K. Mishra (150), Robert B. Riech (188), Roger Kaplan (112) K.K. Saxena (193) and Duglas A.Gray (75) and their findings can be summarised as under.

According to Manfred, entrepreneur should be basically achievement oriented with high degree of creativity, perservance, and imaginative faculties along with risk taking capacity. These basic traits enable them to convert an idea into a project. Taneja identifies urge to control others, self confidence, sense of urgency, superior conceptual abilities, emotional stability, risk taking ability and objective approach as the basic traits along with secondary requirements such as good health and comprehensive awareness about his business. Duncan emphasises problem solving and analytical skills. However Hosmer, Cooper and Vesper say that essential functions of entrepreneur is to recognise commercial potential of an idea, create structures and systems to realise it and then manage it. Mishra quotes a number of studies which have identified the basic traits such as need for achievement (Johnscande 1983), need for power (Stall 1983), leadership styles (Sinha 1980), control orientation (Venkatpathy 1983) work value (Dayal 1980), risk taking capacity (Deivasanpapathy 1980) and high level of aspiration (Kalanidhi &Deivasenpathy 1981). Ritch advocates team management for success. Kaplan says that entrepreneur should also have managerial skills for effective management of their units. Saxena says that innovative style is necessary in fast changing environment. Gray identifies 44 basic traits along with secondary trait such as educational, professional and family background.

Therefore, it can be concluded that Entrepreneurship means high achievement orientation, creativity, perseverance, high imaginative faculties, risk taking ability, control orientation, self confidence, sense of urgency, superior conceptual ability, emotional stability, objectivity, analytical and problem solving skills, ability to recognise commercial potential of ideas, leadership, managerial skills, work values, high level of aspirations, team spirit, innovative skills alongwith good educational/ professional and family background, good health and comprehensive awareness about his business. In other words managerial skills coupled with risk taking capability and sense of ownership are needed in an entrepreneur to succeed. Therefore, any body trying to start any enterprise with significant public funds must be screened to ensure that he possesses such attributes.

(b) Existing Entrepreneurial Profile

The studies conducted by B.N. Singh (204), Ashok Shukla (202), D.N. Tiwari (226), K.V.R. Chowdhary and B.V.K. Reddy

(40), Manohar U. Desponde (50), P.K.Panda and R.K. Mehar (163), M.K. Mishra (150), Richard P. Toub and Dovish L. Lamb (221) S.V.S. Sharma (198) and B.K. Dixit (53) have been reviewed and the results are as under.

B.N. Singh who studied units of Kaval towns of U.P., concludes that trading communities were main sources of entrepreneurship and most of them were not technical. Shukla who studied the units of Varanasi found that 80% of the entrepreneurs were below 40 years of age at the times of establishment of their units. However he also confirms dominance of Vaishya community. He further confirms that most of them were well educated (graduates and above). However, he has found that Brahmins and Khatriya have done better than Vaishyas due to entrepreneurial and risk taking abilities. Tiwari confirms the finding of Shukla with regard to age and education and finds that only 25% of them had exposure to any management programme. Most of them were from well to do families with monthly income above Rs. 3000. Further most of them were autocratic and money making was there basic motive. K.V.R. Chawdhary and B.V.K. Reddy highlight the lack of effective training and orientation to entrepreneurs. Deshpande who studied 90 units of three cities of Maharashtra, found that 60% of the entrepreneurs were local, mostly from trading and other higher castes. Most were young (Average age 32years) and 80% started units with the help of family. He says that similar pattern is also visible is U.S.A. and other countries in respect of small business. He has further reported that local entrepreneurs were mostly engaged in traditional lines, had profit motives, mostly sole proprietorship concerns, thin seed capital/margin money and 72% produced consumer goods. He has also reported that average implementation period was 13 months and better educational background hardly helped in quick implementation and hardly any tangible help from any government agency was visible. He found that 72% of the units were operating below optimal level. P.K. Panda and

R.K. Mehar found that most of the entrepreneurs were from middle/high class from urban areas, majority being graduate and above, 82% of the firms proprietorships and most of them lacking managerial and technical skills and integrity. M.K. Mishra concludes that entrepreneurs of successful units are participative and had faith in ability of their employees. Taub and Lamb interviewed 200 units of Punjab, Orissa and Tamilnadu to find inter regional differences and found that in Punjab entrepreneurs were mostly skills based, in Orissa traditional and the Tamilians were educated unemployed but all had profit motives. S.V.S. Sharma also supports the money motives when he says that castes/class with high monetary values such as Jews, Marwaries and Chettiyars have done better than others. He also supports Despande about better performance of migrants.

Dixit who studied 101 units of Bellary distt. of Karnataka, also found that majority of the entrepreneurs come from trading community and lack managerial and technical skills. They also lack integrity and commitment.

Thus, it is clear that most of the studies have confined themselves to the background of the entrepreneurs rather than analysis of their basic psychological traits mentioned in the preceding para. However it can be concluded that majority of them lack technical and managerial skills and few also lacked integrity and commitment.

(c) Personality Problems of Entrepreneurs

Researcher has reviewed the studied conducted by Vries (143), D.E. Gumpert and P.P Boyd (78), Taneja (220), Neil C Churchil and Verginia L. Levis (41), Duncun (54), Desponde (50) Saxena (193) and Dixit (53) and the results are as under.

Vries finds that entrepreneur are normally egoist and dislike routine, do not want to be told and as such should be handled with care. Grumpert and Boyd says that entrepreneurs are always under tension due to loneliness and are not is a position to ease out their tension due to non existence of friends with whom they could share their problems. They can share them with their advisors. Taneja says that they should learn to manage, trust and delegate and should control their ego. Duncan says that brain storming can help in taking good decision. Despande finds that financial constraints with small entrepreneurs do not permit them to hire full time management experts as such they should engage management persons on part time basis. Mishra says that low level of achievement motives, power needs, risk taking ability, aspirations along with autocratic styles, negative work values, old age and lack of managerial and technical skills lead to failures. Saxena blames government for allowing entry of incompetent entrepreneurs to set up units with public funds. He further says that these units are not able to adopt to fast changing environments and become sick. Dixit also emphasises lack of integrity and commitment.

A review of ideal traits, existing profiles and personality problems indicates that though most of the small entrepreneurs are well educated, well to do and young but they lack basic entrepreneurial, managerial and technical skills required for successful conception, implementation and operation of small scale enterprises on their own.

2.2. THE SUPPLIER GROUP — MANAGEMENT CONSULTANTS AND THEIR ASSOCIATION

2.2.1 Management Consultancy Services — The Evolution

Consultancy service is one of the oldest profession. Herman Holtze (89) states that there has been no time in recorded history when consultants have not been in evidence. It has grown steadily over the years to face growing socio-economic challenges for improving management standards and skills. However, it professionally started in 1888 i.e. more than 100 years back when F. Gilbreth modified the process of brick laying after conducting work study. Amongst the early pioneers were Charls Samson, Frederick Taylor, Frank and Lillion Gilbreth, Arthur D. Little and Edword Booz, all Americans. Therefore, origins of management consultancy are essentially Anglo- American and main role then was to help manufacturing companies become more productive and efficient. They were called industrial engineers and time and motion men. This picture prevailed up to 1960s. However management consultancy was first established in 1926 in U.S.A.. Up to 50's and 60's mostly solo practice was in vague. Now we have big firms like Anderson Consultancy, Mc Kinsey and co., KPMG, Deloittle Touche Tomatsu, Cooper and Lybrand, Aurther Anderson, Price Waterhouse, Booz, Allen and Hamilton, A.T. Kearney, IBM, Boston Consultancy Group and brain and co. In India Tata Consultants and A. F. Fergusion started management consultancy divisions in late sixties. It has been estimated by the Economist (6) that in 1988, there were about 1 lakh consultants world over with annual billing of $10 billion as against $3 billion in the year 1980. In 1995 the word market was likely to be 50 millions sterling pounds and it is growing very fast @ 20% per annum. In U.S alone consultancy firms employed 60,000 consultants. M.D.I study (142) indicates that in Japan alone there were 35,000 consultants in 1984 serving only the small medium enterprises. Therefore global strength of management consultants is difficult to determine because of the confusion about the scope of management consultancy services.

The genesis of industrial/management consultancy services in India dates back to the period immediately after independence i.e. 50's,, when India embarked upon a programme of planned industrial development. In early 50's projects were implemented mostly by foreign consultants. But soon it was realised that development of indigenous consultancy is essential for industrial development of the country. As a result IIMs, IITs, IIPA, ASCI, and IIFT etc were established by the Govt. to develop technical and managerial expertise. Also a expert penal was set up by Govt. of India (planning commission) in 1970 which recommended that an all India body of consultants should be set up to foster healthy development of this profession in the country. Accordingly National Association of Consulting Engineers (NACE) was set up in the year 1976. ILO study (1972) indicates that there were hardly 300 consultants in 1972 and this strength went to 6000 in the year 1978 as per the estimates of the Management Consultants Association of India (MCAI), now named as Institute of Management Consultants of India (IMCI).

Over the years the number of management consultants has been growing and the range of services being offered by them is also widening. However it was only towards the beginning of 80's that consultancy gained momentum. Today the consultancy profession has achieved self-reliance. High quality management consultancy services are being offered by the faculty members of the Management Institutes, members of management consultancy firms, management consultancy divisions of Chartered Accountancy firms and large business groups. Many of them are also registered with international agencies.

DSIR study conducted by NPC (157) (1990), has indicated that there were approximately 500 management consultancy firms employing about 10,000 consultants with estimated turn-over of Rs 250 Crores. MDI study (173) (1994) also confirms the units of management consultancy firms but say that these were 10,000 individual consultants having 'celebrity' status, having good knowledge and experience. It has been further estimated by NPC that 1000 to 1200 i.e. 10% consultants are added each year. Thus we can safely assume that this profession has mostly developed in last 30 years (POST 1970s).

However according to R. Jaganathan (97), there is not a single consultancy firm in India whose annual turn-over cross Rs.100 millions as against $ 5300 millions annual revenue of Anderson Consultancy in the year 1996. The annual billing of A.F. Fergusion and co. from management consultancy was hardly Rs. 30 million and he estimates annual billing of Rs. 500 million with 3000 consultants in the year 1989 as against Rs.2500 millions estimated by NPC for the year 1990. Thus there is lot of confusion about the strength of management consultants in India. This is probably due to confusion about scope of services a management consultant should offer. Institute of Management Consultants of India, Mumbai (IMCI) in particular and Consultancy Development Centre, New Delhi (CDC) in general are responsible for development of management consultancy profession in India. CDC aims at identifying the future consultancy needs and develop consultancy on that lines. Apart from these services, it maintains data base on consultants which can be used by industrial units in general and SSI units in particular. IMCI is also not able to develop quality consciousness in management consultants due to lack of proper authority. Therefore management consultancy profession in India still has miles to go before it can catch up with developed countries.

2.2.2 Basic Features of Management Consultancy Services on International Level

On the basis of the review of related literature, the basic features of management consultancy can be summarised as under.

(a) Consultancy firms could be classified into strategy consultants, general traditional management consultants, accountancy firms, information technology consultants and human relation consultants.

(b) The annual rate of growth in number of management consultants may be around 20%, fastest being in information technology (50%).

(c) There is general lack of effective regulations and quality controls due to non-mandatory nature of controls, leading to low reputation and trustworthiness of management consultants all over the world. Regulation are stricter in developed countries and relaxed in developing countries. Bansal (11) indicates unwillingness on the part of consultants to be regulated by their institute like ICAI for CAs.

(d) There is lack of uniform understanding as what constitutes management consultancy. Strategy consultants disown accountancy firms and all disown recruiters.

(e) To beat their competitors, they require specialists with general management aptitudes. However, small clients still require all in one consultants. So consultants have to choose a market segment.

(f) Reputation is purely based on quality of service and customer's satisfaction.

(g) There is general trend towards mergers to provide integrated services through a wider network but small firms still need small/solo consultants.

(h) Consultancy varies from technical to strategy, functional consultancy lying in between (Calvest Markhana 35).

(i) Size of consultancy firms is very large in developed countries such as USA and UK where 14 firms employed above 1000 consultants each and 23 firms had more than 100 consultants each in the year 1990, the annual consultancy turnover single firm going up to $ 5300 in the year 1996 in case of Anderson Consultancy. However, in developing countries size is much smaller.

(j) Due to increased competition consultancy firms are forced to employ low paid research associates (Shankar Suryanarayan 219).

(k) With regards to the potential area of consultancy, review of existing literature reveal that franchises (Riplay Hotch 91), public sector (Mushkat Miron

154), local self govt. with considerable amount of inefficiency and waste (R.J.Revell 187), information technology (V.M.Sundaram 218), strategy consultancy (Bharat Krishna 119), (Paye A. 167, Mushkat Miron 154), organisational change and development (Dharni P. Sinha 52, Richard Bechard 15, Gunner Hjelhott 88, Robert R.Blacke and Jane Srygley 25, Allen R. Cohen, Stephen Fink &Herman Goden 5, Rolf P. Lyuton 137) and W.Warner Burke 33) and productivity are most promising areas in addition to the traditional business consultancy.

2.2.3 Quality Dimensions of Management Consultancy Services

Quality of service of any consultant depends upon personal competence of the consultant, effectiveness of the selection procedure, extent of use by the client, cost of service, consultant's style, implementation strategies, quality control mechanism and general environmental factors. It is also essential to review other general aspects such as functions, area of consultancy and problems being faced by both the consultants and the clients. Therefore, literature related to above aspects has been reviewed and the result can be summarised as under.

(a) Personal characteristics of management consultant

In order to ascertain the quality of a good consultant, articles of S.S.Varadan (231), Nirmal Singh (205), Golden Godfrey (72), R.T.Golembiewski (73), Management Accounting (141), Cash William B. and Minter Robert L. (36), Jacobson (100) and Donald H. Dunn (55) have been reviewed and it is seen that time consciousness (231), in depth knowledge of the field along with urge to update and adopt to changes, ability to take objective and integrated view, creativeness and innovation, ability to train and impart knowledge, entrepreneurship, vision and participate style, ability to resolve conflict, reliability and optimism for improvement (205), ability to work as neutral participant observer, belief in human potential, populist tendency and ability to unearth hidden motives of the client (73) problem solving ability (145), ability to sell and market and diversified skills for stable income are essential attributes. Jacobson has listed 32 items which could be rated on a 0 to 5 scale and if the average rating is 4 or above without any I or 2, then one can succeed in consultancy practice. Donand H. Dunn (55) also lists similar items and says that hardly 30% of the consultants are in a position to earn full time. He says that consultants must have reasonable financial support, house, telephone and supporting family before starting as a consultant. One should first start on part time basis with some friend. According to him full competency and references are also essential. According to the researcher these attributes are quite challenging and may have to be developed.

(b) Selection of consultants

It is essential to select suitable consultant for quality of consultation work, as such the quality of selection process will directly influence the quality of consultancy service. A number of authors have studied this aspect but the researcher has reviewed the articles of J. Bird (24), Lyle William G. and Rates D.L. (136), Corrin T.J. and Fisher T.K. (44), Lawric Laywood and Urs E. Gittiker (127 &128), S.A. Weises (237), L.L Axton (8), Benard Liebawitz (131), William J. Eibis (62), Herman Holtze (89), A.Jay (103), Howard H. Stenvention and William A. Sahlan (215), and Herbert Hubben (93) and the result is as under.

The main attributes to be considered are, past track record, speed of delivery, personal chemistry, and investment in skill development, to be consulted with old clients. (24), reputation (136), benefits vis-a-vis cost of consultation (44), value system of the consultants (127), consultation with old clients and friends (232), consultant's style (131), size of consultancy firm (103), references from old clients and other general consultants (215). Also, consultant should be hired at an early stage (103), objective analysis of the problems to be done by the entrepreneurs before deciding type of consultant required (131).

(c) Dimensions of consultant's job

In order to ascertain as what a consultant is expected to do during the consultation process, the articles of Ronald Lippit (133) and Harry Blustain (28), have been reviewed. According to Lippit the process of consultation has following dimensions.

(1) A diagnostic theory to identify the real problems of the client.
(2) The extent of involvement of the consultant (style).
(3) Identification of forces for and against the probable changes.
(4) Evaluate his capacity to solve the problem and then continue (frank admission of his inability).
(5) Convince the client and his people that they require change.
(6) Must set clear cut phases of consultation process.
(7) Must leave behind a client who should now know how to
   (a) Cope with similar problems in future.
   (b) Identify future problems and choose a right help.
   (c) Adopt to changing environment.

Lippit further discusses the diagnostic orientation which can be either disproportionate distribution of power or blocking of productive energy, inadequate communication, lack of comparison with the standards, i.e. control system, lack of goal clarity and lack of decision making ability. He has developed following stages with Watson and Wetley.

(1) Develop need for change.
(2) Establish consulting relationships.
(3) Clarification of client's problems.
(4) Examine alternative solutions and goals.
(5) Transformation of intentions into actual change efforts.
(6) Stabilisation of new group functions.
(7) Termination of consulting relationship.

Blustain says that the consultant should be able to obtain full faith of the client like the Shaman. Most of the problems may be of social and psychological nature than of technical nature and as such good demonstration ability gives alternative vision. Psychology plays major role in consultant and client relationship.

(d) Consultancy Styles

Consultancy style also influences the quality of consultation work. As such in order to ascertain the spectrum of consultants' styles, the studies done by Dharni P. Sinha (52), Udai Parikh (164), Iswar Dayal (48), S.E. Devid (51), Metzer R.O. (148), Mcdonald Edwin D. (146), G.L. Lippit (132), Sreedhar Raghavan (176) and Bianco V.E. (22) have been reviewed and the result is as under.

Lippit prescribes a continuum of consultancy styles based on directional intensity on the part of the consultant. It is minimum in case of reflector and maximum in case of doctor and in between lie process specialists, fact finders, alternative identifiers, educators, trainers and technical experts in increasing order. According to him, consultants require a lot of tact, politeness, trust and friendliness to unearth the real intentions of not only the client but his people also.

Sinha identifies three types of interventions experiential, process and structured. Under the first model the intentions are to be understood, and steps to be suggested to remove mis-understandings to improve people's capability. Under the process model the consultant only works as a catalyst and help the client and his people to do whatever consultant do himself in the first model. Under the structured model the consultant is result oriented and controlled. He diagnose the problems and suggest remedial actions and also helps in implementation.

Parekh also advocates for the process model and says that consultant should facilitate client organisations in understanding the dynamics of various processes and deciding improvements themselves by developing in house capability and should not make them dependent on him. According to him it is always better to respect client's values and have flexible and tentative approach, understand organisational politics, sell ideas softly, understand the need perception of client clearly and have intensive interaction with the client and his people.

Dayal also prefers process style and is of the view that the consultant should enable client to face future problems on their own. However he places emphasis on detailed planning for management of change. Devis also feels that consultant should be able to awaken client's faith in future. Raghavan is of the view that big organisations should develop in house consultancy capability with the help of external consultants. Participative style has been advocated by R.O. Metzer.

Thus, it is evident from the above that style relates to the degree of participation of client and the consultant in the consultation process. However it may be seen that the SSI units are mostly one man show and there is not much of organisational politics and the consultants has to keep the entrepreneur in confidence.

(e) Utilisation of consultants

Best use of the consultants' capabilities will lead to better quality. In order to understand this process, the studies of Herman Holtze (89), A. Jay (103), Sharu S. Ragnekar (181), Norris Devid B. (160) and Howard H Stevension and William A. Sahlman (215) have been reviewed and the result is as under:

Client has to understand unit's problems quite well (may be with the help of a consultant) and then only go for suitable consultant. Second the consultancy contract should define the expectations of both the parties very clearly and implementation should be emphasised. This is essential for mutual faith and trust. Client should understand the rationale the fee being charged (89). Consultant has to be integrated with the management team, closely controlled and the client has to see that he does not offer impractical suggestions with the help of raw/junior consultants which he might have employed. However he must refrain from undue interference in consultation process (103). Periodical reviews (181), clear agreement and complete meeting of minds (160), tough minded negotiations of terms and conditions, demanding reasons for recommendations (215) are also essential.

Thus it is seen that complete understanding of each other's expectations, faith and mutual trust, active participation and periodical review with due emphasis on implementation are major pre-requisites for optimal utilisation of a consultant.

(f) Consultant-client Relationship

It is futile to expect quality work unless a positive and fruitful relationship is developed between both the parties. In order to appreciate various facets of this relationship, the studies of Dharni P. Sinha (52), Richard Beckhard (15), R. C. Teneyek (223), T. Moline (227), Glassman Alan M. and others (71), Golembiewski R. T. (73), Grang C. Lundlerg (135), J.S.Landlorio (126) and Pedro J. Pech (172) have been reviewed and the result is as under:

Sinha prescribes four models of interaction depending upon degree of involvement, i.e., collaborative, clinical, engineering and survival models. Under the first, problems and goals etc. are identified through mutual consultation and both learn in this process, consultant working as facilitator. In the clinical model client (patient) does exactly as told by the consultant (doctor) and client's involvement is minimum. However under engg. Model, the supplier of services (consultant) has to follow the commands of the purchaser of services (client). As such involvement of consultant in minimum. Under the fourth model, the consultant is thrust upon by the third party (bank etc.), as such both parties have passive roles and the relations are forced and cool (52).

According to Bechhard, relationship is dependent upon factors such as dependency of client on the consultant, elements of suspicion and mistrust, degree of threat to existing power structure, traditions in the client's organisation and resultant resistance, pressure of client for early results, confusion in the minds of clients' people about the power position of the consultant, unrealistic expectations on the part of client and his people about the results and their own involvement in the consultation process, low connection in the minds of the organisational leaders about the needs and actions desired on their part. He is of the view that most of the above can be managed by active participation and frank discussions and entering into a clearly framed consultancy contract with the consent of all concerned.

Teneyck discusses the time frame of this relationship and is of the opinion that quality work, close rapport with the client and his people, alertness to future signs of problems and frequent contact with the client even after termination of the relationships make these relations reliable and durable (223). Researcher has tried to assess the deepness of the relationship by asking a question whether the client will like to repeat the same consultant for future consultation.

A survey (73) of 27 consultants conducted to know the elements of successful consultancy, reveals that strong client's commitment, clear understanding of the power relationships (formal as well as informal) obtaining in client's organisation and its management are the critical factors. Other pre-requisites are clear understanding of each other's expectations, need based consultancy strategy, mutual faith and trust, effective communication between both the parties, active participation of the client and his people and adequate fee.

Another survey (71) of 20 OD consultants has also identified positive elements such as clarity in roles / contract, mutual trust and respect, competence of consultant, high degree of client's commitment and frequent exchange of information.

Lundlerg discusses the application of transactional analysis to consultant-client relationship and says that in clinical model the consultant (doctor) is in parent ego state and the client (patient) in child ego state. In the collaborative model both are in adult ego state. Normally most of these transactions are complementary in nature, but some time they become crossed due to lack of trust which is quite possible in survival model due to forced relationships. (135).

Landlorio says that maintaining secrecy of the information provided by the client and his people is the key element of a healthy relationship and once information is leaked, the whole relationship gets vitiated due to breach of trust. Also positive perception about consultant's character and personal reporting to client are a must for building positive relationships, which can be used to generate further business if rising stars are marked well in advance.

Thus, it is seen that consultant-client relationship depends on degree of quality and duration of involvement. Healthy relations are essential for successful practice. Researcher has tried to know the quality of relationship by examining the duration of relationship and possibility of repeat engagement.

(g) Pre-requisites for successful implementation of recommendations

Success of implementation depends upon the quality of recommendations, their presentation and the co-operation of the client and his people who matter. In order to identify the various pre-requisites, the articles of Jr. of management consultancy (107), W.P.Hall (80), Jay Bary (17), Allen W. (238), Tindley Devis (225) and Petro J. Peck (172) have been reviewed and the results are as under:

Gradual approach from most painful area (which also gives quick results) to other more difficult areas capable of giving results in long run, leads to better reception by the clients and their people as the benefits come to their notice quite early (107). Good project management facilitates realistic diagnosis and early recommendations (80). Good human relations and interpersonal skills on the part of consultant is also essential for getting full co-operation of the client and his people in identifying real perceptions of all concerned to enable the consultant to diagnose the problems properly and offer practical suggestions and for obtaining their further co-operation in implementing these suggestions (17). Consultants should always select an area and should concentrate more on the results than report writing (238).

Quality of service is dependent on the degree to which client's actual needs are met and once a client is convinced about the utility and likely benefits of the recommendations, he himself will facilitate their implementation. Meaningful recommendations are not possible unless the consultant is able to understand the nature and status of client's business, politics of client's organisation, listen to all concerned with full attention, have frank discussion with them, manage politics and emphasises on the positive aspects (172). Therefore, quality of recommendation, interpersonal skills and gradual approach may help in implementation.

(h) Marketing strategy

In order to identify the elements of marketing strategy, the articles of Paul N. Bloom (27), Brain P. Smith (211), King Leslie (118), Washburn A. Stewart (235), Shay E. Michael (199), Pierre Guiltel and D.C. Mauthoux (153), J.V.O. Conner (43), Moldenhouer A. Charles (152), Sharon G. Johson (104), Grriel. M. Gelb (76), Charles. F. Harding (82), Sharley J. Feller (64) and W.A. Cohen (42) have been reviewed. Most of the authors are practicing management consultants themselves and have expressed their views on the basis of their own experience.

Increased competition and declining public image has forced management consultants to adopt some marketing strategy to maintain and expand their sales. It is primary responsibility of professional bodies/institutes to create public awareness about roles of consultant and enforce quality by proper regulation to maintain the reputation of the profession and faith of people in this profession. Consultant on his part has to select a market segment depending upon his strength. Bloom identified four types of segment depending upon the size of client's organisation, sophistication level of client's managers and need awareness. Small/medium organisations with unsophisticated managers and unfocused needs have been termed as Pussy Cats and large organisations with same nature as elephants, where as similar organisations with sophisticated managers and focused consultancy needs have been termed as bulldog and tigers. Consultants have to adopt appropriate strategy for a particular segment, meet the requirements, complete the job in time and be in constant touch with the clients to get repeat business from them.

Smith advocates full range of marketing plan i.e. product up-gradation/enrichment/diversification as per needs of selected market segment, good public image, quality of service and constant touch with the clients to get their pulse. Conner also suggests product enrichment by adding discrete capability.

Jonson also emphasises on the need to understand the specific consultancy needs of clients of a particular segment and then develop services accordingly to get their satisfaction and also future business from them. Gelb also feels continuous product (service) development is essential to keep pace with changing needs of market. He also prohibits price war as it spoils the reputation and quality of service.

Washburn feels that arousal of latent needs of customers is essential to generate demand. This can be done by letting him realise his real consultancy needs and once he is aware, he is quite likely to demand it. Michel emphasises need for effective brochures/publicity materials to increase clients' awareness. Mauthoux recommends anti-bureaucratic consultancy organisation to maintain personal satisfaction of the member consultant so that they could do effective personal selling.

Moldenhauer suggests that only the top man of the potential client organisation should be contacted through letters seminars and intensive follow up. Cohen also advocates use of seminar/articles in professional journals.

Harding conducted survey of 50 consultants to identify their marketing strategy and he has identified four models i.e. builders, artists, miners and the sellers. The builders capitalise on existing relationships to get additional business through reference strategy. Artists heavily depend upon personal selling without any market plan. Miners over cultivate existing relationships to get more business from the same clients by adding more products/services. However the sellers have a well planned marketing strategy. Feller also advocates focused area and right publicity.

Thus, it is primary responsibility of the Consultants' Associations/Institutes to create awareness amongst the customers about the utility of management consultancy services. However consultants on their part have to select a market segment based on their individual expertise, achieve full client satisfaction and be in touch with the clients for repeat business, continuously upgrade/enrich their services as per changing market needs to be ascertained through market surveys, arousal of latent consultancy needs of customers, personal selling through seminar and contact at the top, to increase their business. Researcher has tried to know the conditions prevailing in India.

(i) Pricing and Engagement Strategy

Consultants could be engagement on the retainership basis or for a specific job. However the methods applied to calculate consultancy charges may differ. In this connection articles of Jr. of management consultancy (110), Shankar Suryanarayan (219), Taveggia Thomos (222), Bloom Fracklin B. (26), Bloom Paul N. (27) and Main J. (140) have been reviewed and the result is as under:

A survey (110) of 113 assignments done by consultants revealed that the clients who had engaged consultants on retainership basis, were less satisfied than those who engaged only for a specific job. However this finding has been contradicted by Bloom (27) who says that once client is satisfied that he is getting more than he is paying and scope of services included in the retainership package are well defined, then the retainership is the best arrangement for small firms. But the consultant has to understand the client and his business well and involve him fully through constant touch to enable him to give effective suggestions on continuous basis.

Value of advice (price), depends upon capability and needs of the client and accordingly it may be fixed (219). It also depends on quality of service and state of competition (140). The charge for consultant man days depends upon the salary of consultant likely to be used, portion of overheads and estimated annual consultant hours likely to be charged (222). The price should not be used as a marketing tool, as it affects the quality of service and the reputation of the consultant adversely.

(j) Structure of management consultancy organisations

In order to see as what type of structure is most suited for management consultancy organisations to enable them to give quality services, articles of Weld Coxe (45), N.Krishnamoorthy (120), Nirmal Singh (205), Narendra Mohinder (151), Cash William B. (36) and Lorsch Jay. W. and Pelter F. Maithias (134) have been reviewed and the results are as under:

Structure of an organisation should match its nature of business (45). Consultancy organisation should be flat type with two or three layers, anti-bureaucratic, have autonomous units, highly conscious, quick responsive to customer's demands, innovative and flexible, and small in size (120). Also, management of consultancy firms should provide an atmosphere in which consultants feel free to give their best and have inherent urge to grow. This is only possible in a small informal organisation.

According to Nirmal Singh 60% of the consultancy firms are one man show and about 15% have 2 to 5 consultants. Narendra Mahindra says that consultancy firm normally employ three types of employees i.e. doers, those who gather data, analyse and draft reports under the supervision of middle level consultants, middle level consultants who partly guide doers and partly do personal selling and lastly the sellers who arrange business for the firm, run the organisation and decide its policies. However it may be true for big firms. The sellers have to set goals, select suitable consultants, watch their works and evaluate them. This has been also supported by Cash who says that consultancy organisation have normally 3 tiers of Junior consultants, Managers and Vice Presidents or Directors. They also have project team structure. Normally working capital problem is major problem and as such a tight controls on cash flows is a must.

Thus, it is seen that consultancy organisation should be small, flat type, flexible, adoptive, and quality conscious. Researcher has attempted to evaluate these attributes in the existing organisation through field survey.

2.2.4 Problems of Management Consultants

In order to have a general idea about the problems being faced by management consultants, the articles of Arnold Putman (7), Nirmal Singh (205 &206), V. Kumar (122), Dharni P. Sinha (52), N.B.Grant (74), Miller Ernest. C. (149), Economist (60), T.Moline (227), W.L Brocknan (30), R. Kanh (189), J. P. Frankenhus (111) Journal of management consultancy (109) and Robert H. Guest (77), have been reviewed and the problems identified by these authors have been summarised as under:

(1) Mistrust of client on the consultants (206).

(2) The clients consider expenditure on consultancy fee as wastage and are unwilling to pay proper fee (206).

(3) Lower payment capacity of smaller units (206).

(4) Acute shortage of good quality consultants capable of solving the problems of the clients to their satisfaction (206).

(5) Allergy of top management towards consultants due to ego and lack of professionalism (122).

(6) Low demand for consultancy services leading to viability problem and resultant cash flow problems and tendency of consultants to indulge in sub-standard work on lower fee (122)).

(7) Lack of data on consultancy needs as well as on the services available (122 and 205).

(8) Very few consultants serving the small scale sector due to viability problems (60).

(9) Frequent changes of the decision makers in the client's organisation (205).

(10) No survey done so far either by the IMCI or Industry Associations to know the feed back of the users about the quality of service (149).

(11) Consultants not willing to be controlled by their institute with regard to quality of service or professional ethics (102).

(12) Use of outdated concepts/methods by consultants and lack of adaptability (60).

(13) Absence of proper training and development for consultants (189).

(14) Mis-understanding between consultants and clients due to vague consultancy contracts (227).

(15) Lack of desired level of involvement of the clients or/and their people leading to impractical suggestions (111).

(16) Mishandling of assignments by Jr. consultants due to improper supervision by Senior consultants (109).

(17) Failure on the part of consultants in anticipating consequences of their recommendations including the likely changes in the pattern of conflicts (109).

(18) Inability to understand the real intentions of the client and his people including the politics going on , by the consultants and subsequent difficulty in getting the recommendations implemented (109).

(19) Failure of clients to utilise the services of the consultant optimally due to ego problem including desired participation in the consultation process.

Thus, it is evident that consultants are basically facing problems of personal and organisational weakness coupled with low demand of their service from the clients due to mistrust and lack of awareness. The researcher has attempted to identify the gaps in demand and supply including policies and practices.

2.2.5 Basic features of management consultancy services in India

Basic features of management consultancy services in India as summarised by NPC study (157) and MDI study (173) 1994 are as under:

(a) Unlike in developed countries, manufacturing sector is the main user (75%) in India whereas in developed countries service sector is main user.

(b) Major areas of use are marketing, (including market surveys), feasibility studies and corporate strategy.

(c) Annual consultancy turnover varies between 0.50 lakhs to 3.5 lakhs between partnership and private limited companies, daily consultation fee per consultant varying between Rs 200 to Rs 7500 depending upon competence and reputation of the consultant and ability of client to pay.

(d) Most of the consultants (80%) are concentrated in the metropolitan cities.

(e) Annual turnover from management consultancy has been estimated to be around Rs 2500 millions during 1993-94 (173).

(f) India is providing far lesser subsidy towards meeting the cost of consultants than even developed countries.

(g) Consultants promote their sales mostly by repeat performance (73%), through friends and relatives (14%), image and reputation (14%) and usual marketing (3%). In other words there is no conscious marketing efforts. However major marketing tools adopted are lectures/seminars (70%) and enlistment/empenelment with financial institutions (33%) like consultants of developed countries.

(h) Major methods adopted to identify problems are

discussions with the clients (89%), diagnostic studies (21%) and as told by the clients (21%). Involvement of clients or their representatives was found to be at stages (48%), continuous (42%), through coordination (23%), and only in implementation (6%) which indicates fair degree of involvement.

(i) Methods used to sell recommendations were involvement of clients (71%), final report (34%), selling to top management (29%) and participation in the implementation (6%).

(j) Method of charging consultancy fee were based on consultant's man days (83%) and ad hoc (10%), whereas in other countries fee is also charged percentage of savings and on retainership basis also.

(k) Consultants are recruited mostly from reputed management institutes and not from competitors and it is seen that 50% of the consultants have experience of 5 years or less, 25% between 5 and 10 years and remaining over 10 years.

(l) Remuneration pattern indicates that only 8% of them are being paid well over the industry average, 21% above industry average, 41% at par but remaining below industry average. Thus, it is seen that remuneration is not good may be due to lack of demand or low calibre but the study is silent on this.

(m) Major factors motivating to excel are self development (47%), out of turn promotion (37%), bonus (31%), sharing of surplus (24%) and training abroad (10%).

(n) There is a general consensus that the quality control on management consultants in India is very poor by the IMCI due to voluntary nature of control.

2.2.6 Various dimensions of management consultancy services for Small Scale sector at the global level

In order to ascertain the various dimensions of management consultancy for the SSI sector the articles of P.N.L. Raju (178), P.Chattopadhaya (39), Malcolm Harper (84), R. M. Khajuria (114), SISI Bombay (209), S.S.Badekar (10), SISI Bangalore (208), A.K.Mahapatra (138), P.C.Patnayak (169), SDEME (195), MDI (142), Jr. of general management (106), G.B.Jakodia (101), U.V.Bhatta (18), Braker J.S. (29), Curisman J.J. (46), Bratice E. Hamilton and Preston G. Smith (81), William M. Carson and William N. Head (87), John Block Ford (65), Sharod Nelton (159), Devid M. freeman (66), Peck Richardson J. (170) and S. N. Bidani and P.K. Mishra (23), have been reviewed. Most of the above authors are practicing management consultants to the small scale industry. Therefore, they are expected to be aware of the basic feature of this profession.

(1) According to Raju, demand from the SSI sector is restricted to preparation of feasibility/project reports for obtaining financial assistance from financial institutions/ banks and for completing other formalities. Demand for consultancy to solve implementation and other post production problems is very low due to lack of awareness about utility of management consultancy and hardly any trust in them. He also confirms that quality of management consultants is really very bad. He said that the TCOs have mostly restricted themselves to project consultancy. Chattopadhaya feels that small units require more help in the area of procedures and systems than larger units. He feels that one consultant can serve about 50 SSI units fruitfully.

(2) Harper concentrates on the cost of consultancy and based on his own experience and he recommends that young unemployed graduates from colleges/universities could be employed after training them for three weeks. They can work as bare foot consultants, to provide consultancy at a cost SSI units can afford. He also confirms that one bare foot consultant

can solve day to day problems of 50 to 60 units located in one area thus conforming the figure given by Raju. He further says that one supervisory consultant can control 4 to 5 such bare foot consultants and the project leader can supervise 4 to 5 such field supervisors. Thus one project leader can assist 1000 to 1250 small units in a region. Harper has already experimented it in Kenya, Brazil, Sri Lanka and Indonesia and has obtained good results. He has noticed a tendency in entrepreneur of SSI units to blame lack of resources for all their ills. However the actual analysis done by him revealed that real problems were lack of costing, managerial inefficiency, and expensive ways of doing things. This, according to him, is due to poor education and geographical isolation of the entrepreneurs. He feels that the entrepreneurs can be trained to change their negative and escapist approach and enable them to see their problems in their right perspectives. He further says that main job of consultant is to diagnose root cause and then recommend simple recommendations which could be easily implemented by the clients without additional finance. He feels that highly qualified consultants may hardly like to service SSI units due to economy and interaction problems. According to him financial analysis is the starting point after the problem of mistrust is solved. The emphasis has to be on cost reduction and optimal use of existing resources before going for any additional investment. He further feels that such bare foot consultants can be evaluated on the basis of number of clients served, nos. of recommendations given, nos. of recommendations accepted and the end resultsf.

(3) Lack of demand for management consultancy has been confirmed by Khajuria also and according to him, lack of expertise appropriate to the needs of SSI units is prime reason along with other reasons. However apart from project consultancy productivity/profitability analysis and rehabilitation of sick units are main areas of usage. He feels that govt. must encourage this profession for the benefit of SSI sector in the national interest.

(4) SISIs are mostly engaged in on the spot study and advice, integrated plant/productivity studies and market surveys (208 and 209). At present all emphasis is on pre-production problems and the post-production problems are being neglected. The other problems are poor quality of consultants, neglect of rural areas, inadequate training facilities of entrepreneurs, and scarce data on small units. SISI studies have suggested that management/ business consultancy should be linked with financial assistance. The consultancy wings of SISIs may be made independent and all govt./ semi- govt./Pvt. consultants may be coordinated by state directorate of industries.

(5) Bedekar also confirms that TCOs have mostly confined themselves to project/industrial consultancy except for GITCO and KITCO and he also feels their activities should be coordinated. Bhatt also confirms this pattern and recommends for their restructuring to provide management consultancy services to small scale sector.

(6) Mahapatra emphasises that the consultancy needs of SSI units are integrated and undifferentiated. He feels that normally the healthy units have focused needs and can hire consultants even from other cities but struggling units face financial and marketing problems and require cooperation of banks etc. The unborn units require industrial and project consultancy. He further elaborates consultancy needs of SSIs at different stages of operations like other authors quoted earlier and says that pre-operational needs are entrepreneurial training, procedural and other guidance including financing etc. Take off needs include design of systems in all functional areas of management and formulation of management strategies in different fields like finance, marketing and production etc. The post operational needs are normally the problems arising in different areas with regards to failures to achieve pre-determined objectives. The unit may like to expand its operations and may again need techno-managerial

assistance. However, if the unit become sick then it require complete diagnostic and techno-managerial package which may require approval of financial institutions if additional finance is involved. He also identifies their major problems to be geographical spread, confusion about their real needs, distrust on consultants and improper record keeping. He suggest that the FIs should install effective monitoring system to identify problematic units at an early stage and hand over such units to TCOs/SISIs/NPC/PVT. Consultants for diagnostic study and suggesting remedial measures. A complete data base for management consultants is also required.

(7) Patnayak confirms perception gap between consultants and the clients, incompetence of the owners and viability problem of consultancy firms due to poor payment capacity of the clients and the wide range of expertise required. SEDME reports a case of perception gap which was detected in a case study (195) of a small unit at the instance of UNDP. The client quoted escalation in project cost leading to increase in margin money for fixed assets and resultant shortage of margin money for working capital, erratic power and material supply and high interest burden due to increased loan as the main problems. However actual analysis revealed that main problems were inability to estimate project cost correctly and implement project timely. The other problems were absence of costing system etc. The consultant recommended substitution of raw material to improve its availability, installation of a DG set, improvement in production process to reduce rejections. Thus the hypothesis of Harper of simple solutions was confirmed in this case.

(8) The case studies conducted by MDI have also confirmed that the problems identified by the entrepreneurs were mostly secondary and only partly true. The more critical problems (which they sometimes try to conceal) pertained to in house inefficiency due to conflicts between the partners

leading to delays in implementation of the project, serious technical flaws even in the units promoted by technical entrepreneurs and other managerial mistakes. Though lack of working capital and cost overruns were major secondary problems but primary reason was mismanagement.

(9) National Seminar (1984) on management consultancy services for small scale industries conducted as part of UNDP/ILO project identified constraints such as lack of consultancy culture, more importance to finance than managerial inputs, lack of data on management consultants, late identification of sick units, poor payment capacity of the small units and hesitations in parting with information by the owners. It was also agreed that the quality of services of TCOs is better than SISIs and the services of the consultancy cells of the commercial were mostly restricted to the units financed by them. Also it was general view that private consultants mostly serve larger units due to viability problems. It was further agreed that finance and marketing were most critical areas of consultancy for small units. Experience of GITCO and KITCO could be replicated elsewhere also. Seminar suggested development of solo consultants may be from the retired persons, expansion of consultancy fee subsidy scheme, professionalisation and exchange of the staff of TCO/SISI/NPC's/bank cells, proper training facilities for small business consultants, creating awareness about benefits of management consultancy services through seminars and training, develop skills in the staff of the FIs/Banks to enable them to identify problematic units early, develop bare foot consultants for cheaper services as suggested by Harper, in depth training to the staff of DICs to enable them to provide effective consultation to small units and establishment of a special cell in planning commission to monitor growth of management consultancy profession.

(10) The said seminar also suggested that real consultancy needs of SSI units should be identified along with the agencies which could provide such services clearly highlighting the

gaps in demand and supply. The researcher could not locate any such academic research work for the SSI sector in India.

(11) Carson and Head also confirm that small business management consultants should be generalists with technical experience i.e. degree in science or technology with management /commerce/economics degree and should preferably have about 15 years experience of running a small unit. He feels that having legal orientation will be quite helpful.

(12) Ford also feels that normal consultancy model do not fit for small units. According to him there are only few consultants who can actually solve all the problems of small units. Ford who himself has run a small unit for 20 years, identifies the major problems of small units to be one man show, absence of competent men to help, under capitalisation, general resistance to change, absence of close and confident advisors and personality deficiency in the owner. As such any consultation for small units essentially require total diagnosis and close monitoring of the entire assignment due to over-business of the entrepreneur. Small entrepreneurs are normally egoist and do not wish to avail external help as it will amount to admitting their weakness. Therefore tactful dealing with small entrepreneurs is essential. Normally small business consultants have office cum residence and are assisted by their wife and other unemployed members of their family in day to day work. They only focus on the CEO (mostly entrepreneur) as client and seek long term relationships (retainership) and have long term strategic plans. It is practical to have several small duration meetings with the entrepreneurs than one marathon (long) meeting due to time constraints on their part. Written reports are seldom given and the fee is normally charged on monthly basis. Ford a practicing consultant himself is serving 4 to 5 units from more than 4 years on retainership basis and feels that one can easily serve 6 or 7 units as Part time Chief Finance Officer. He starts from

the most painful area to long term concerns. He has found it difficult to add consultant to assist him due to fear of loosing direct touch with the client and also dilution in the quality of service.

(13) Peck also says that SSIs need simple suggestions which may show quick results. He is of the view that lack of financial and market inputs are basic causes of failure of SSI units. Nelton says that conflict resolution is the main challenge and as such consultant should be chosen after full consultation with the partners or family members as the case may be. The fee should never be the only criterion for selecting a consultant and good consultants with proven track record should be hired. In USA, 20 universities are conducting courses on small business management but in India hardly there is any such course.

(14) Freeman discusses the scope of tailor made services to reduce the cost such as writing business plan and making financial projections etc. He also says that a consultant can work as financial adviser to 5 to 6 firms and gives 4 hours per week per client and give rest of advise on phone. Some big consultants also give consultancy to small unit as subsidised rate in anticipation of getting business when such firms grow in future.

(15) Mishra and Bidani also say that complete diagnosis is a must and simple suggestions for improvement should be given in place of bulky reports having unnecessary data. They also confirm that TCOs are only giving project consultancy.

2.2.7 Management consultancy services for small scale industries in India

As already indicated earlier, small units require management consultancy at five stages i.e pre- production in which knowledge of PERT/CPM and other techniques of production management along with financial optimisation is required, second stage is take off stage in which marketing services are required along with financial planning etc., third phase is post production stage when sound operational decisions are to be taken and implemented, fourth stage is expansion stage in which project consultancy is again called for and lastly the sickness stage where again techno-managerial services are required in a package form. It has been pointed that at all the stages technical consultancy should be linked with management consultancy especially in small units and it should cover all the functional areas.

It is seen that small unit management is mostly one man show and as such performance of the unit is mostly dependent upon the entrepreneurial and managerial capability of the entrepreneur. Also due to financial constraints, it is not possible for him to appoint any full time professional technical/ management expert. Since entrepreneurs fail to solve internal problems of the unit, they tend to blame external factors without accepting their own weakness. Thus consultancy to small units is also related to the personality of the entrepreneur.

Management consultancy for small business in India is still in its embryonic stage. Due to various govt. incentives, the growth of in number of small scale units has been very fast but there has been no matching growth in the number of management consultants for small scale industrial units. NPC study (157) estimates that for every 600 registered SSI units, there is only one management consultant. It is further seen that this profession is ill organised and ill controlled with regard to quality of service as concluded by the seminar on management consultancy for small business held in at Delhi in the year 1984.

The sources of management consultancy services for SSIs are many such as individual consultants, consulting firms, management institutes, management consultancy divisions of the accounting firms, industrial research institutes, technical consultancy organisations (TCO's), SISIs, NPC and District

Industries Centres etc. These could be grouped in three categories i.e. govt., semi- govt. and private consultants.

In govt. sector Small Industry Development Organisation (SIDO) is prominent consultancy organisation set up in the year 1954 by govt. of India. It suggests pattern of industrial development for small scale sector including technical advice. It has 27 Small Industries Service Institutes (SISIs), 31 branch SISIs, 37 SSI extension centres, 4 regional testing centres, 19 field testing centres and a number of production cum process centres/tool rooms etc. It has also allied institutions such as National Small Industries Corporation (NSIC), Central Institute of Tools Design (CITD), Institute of Design for Electrical Measuring Instruments (IDEMI), National Institute of Small Industry Extension and Training (NISIET) and National Institute of Small Business Development (NISBUD). Management consultancy is provided by SISIs in co-ordination with state directorate of industries and others. These services consist of two types i.e. solve specific problem of faced by entrepreneurs by conducting detail in plant studies and arranging training programmes on marketing, finance, costing and production etc. However quality of their services is required to be evaluated. Second set of govt. consultancy organisations are District Industries Centres (DICs) which were started in the year 1978 by the then Janata Govt. At present there are over 432 DICs. No comprehensive data is available on their performance except for 4 case studies conducted by MDI. It is seen that entrepreneurs mostly approach DICs for getting information about various incentives given by the govt. and not for consultation. Therefore they are mostly defunct so far management consultancy is concerned.

Under the category of semi-govt., consultancy organisation, we can include TCOs promoted by FIs/banks, consultancy cells of the commercial banks, and other autonomous bodies. The most important organisation in this category are Technical Consultancy Organisations (TCOs).

After establishment of IBDI in 1964, it was felt necessary to identify promising areas for industrialisation, prepare preliminary feasibility reports, locate suitable managerial and entrepreneurial talents, prepare detail project reports, and finally ensure that required technical, managerial and financial assistance is made available to small scale units which were not capable of doing these activities on their own. Therefore with these objectives in view, TCOs were established from 1976 onwards by the All India financial Institutions in participation with the state govts., state financial and development corporations and the commercial banks. At present there are 18 TCOs in various states, 9 sponsored by IDBI, 5 by IFCI, 3 by ICICI and one by Karnataka Govt., sponsoring institution's share being 51% of the equity capital. Now in some TCOs the share of AIFIs has been diluted. Initially bulk of their business was from the small scale sector but now its share is coming down. Initially they concentrated on industrial consultancy only now they have diverted to the area of management consultancy also. They employ 386 consultants, average employment being 15 ranging from 10 consultants in case of HIMCON to 43 in case of KITCO. Their quality of service has been perceived to be better than SISIs due to autonomy they enjoy. They undertook 4742 consultancy assignments in the year 1991-92 and 296 entrepreneurial development programs in 1992-93. As on 31.3.93, they had handled 45621 assignments (41883 pre-investment studies, 3699 post- investment studies, 39 turn-key assignments) and 45714 persons have been trained by them through 1703 EDPs. But they could hardly give any attention to backward and rural areas and on labour intensive techniques. They are hardly giving any management consultancy except GITCO, KITCO and NEITCO, that too on very small scale. •Second important organisation extending management consultancy service is National Productivity Council with its state and city branches. Though its net work is quite wide but it is mostly serving large and medium scale industries and very few SSIs are being served. Secondly it is mostly concentrating on productivity studies by applying the techniques of industrial engineering and is hardly engaged in other areas of management consultancy. The commercial banks have their own consultancy bureaus but mostly to assist their credit branch in appraising loan proposals and providing consultancy to only those units who have taken loan with a view to recover the loans given to such units. In 1973-74 SBI established a consultancy service cell (CSC) linked to the operation wing of the bank to provide integrated package of services to the small scale units basically who also take loan from the bank. At present SBI has 13 consultancy cells, one each at the local head offices. Further one officer has been provided at the regional offices also. Other commercial banks have also established their own consultancy cells but at a very small scale. These cells are also training their staff in appraising the credit proposals.

The third category of consultants are private consultancy firms, which are mostly small in size and in majority of cases one man show. Large number of consultants are expert in one or two areas only but they are handling assignments in other areas also thus adversely affecting the quality of service. In India starting a consultancy service is very simple process i.e. have an average knowledge, a telephone, a company name, some stationery and a room to sit or even share. Also there are quite a good number of fly by night firms with glamorous names with almost no worthwhile experience. They have been mostly failures in industry/previous jobs and become consultants to pass rough time. This is possible because there is absolutely no restriction on entry of such persons to the consultancy profession either by govt. or any other professional body like IMCI. There are few very good consultants who are in great demand and are cornered by large and medium scale units.They are very costly also say Rs 7500 a day. Thus private consultants are either not competent to solve the management problems of SSIs or have not bothered to look to their side and are busy with larger units who can afford them.

It has already discussed that India in still far behind in use of management consultants. Further it is not known as how many of the management consultants serve small units. MDI study has not replied this question. In India no research has been done on the quality of management consultancy services being given to small scale industrial units. However, researcher has reviewed what ever literature is available on the various possible dimensions of quality and the review has already been summarised above. The findings have kept in mind while talking to the SSIs and the management consultants.

2.2.8 Overall View

Review of related literature reveal that majority of management consultants do not serve small units and as such utilisation of their services by SSIs is quite low. As reported by a number of practicing consultants, a consultant can hardly serve more than 10 units effectively. Thus taking into account the fact that 75% of the 30 lakhs small units are not doing well, India should have more than 200,000 management consultants exclusively for small scale sector on the presumption that if the quality of management consultancy services is reasonably good and the cost could be afforded by SSIs then this sector may utilise the services of such consultants. However at present we have only 15000 consultants majority of them are not management consultants and also do not serve SSIs even when they are working well. Therefore, this phenomenon requires in-depth study. Since the literature survey indicates the problems of bad quality of consultancy, higher cost of service, lack of professionalism on the part of SSI entrepreneurs and lack of awareness about the benefits of management consultancy services etc. have been reported to be prime reasons behind lower utilisation, it may be academically rewarding to study the quality dimensions of management consultancy services available for SSI sector.

3

Current Features and Perception of the Supplier Group—The Management Consultants/Their Associations

The object of this study is to appraise the quality dimensions of Management Consultancy Services available to Small Scale Industrial Units (SSIs) in India. The quality dimensions related to the suppliers of service (consultants and their association) are size and culture of the consultancy organisations, academic/professional and experience profiles of consultants, management problems of the clients, type of services being made available vis-à-vis the real consultancy deeds of the clients, mode of fee being charged and mode of engagement/continuity of relationship etc. Also the reasons for not serving SSIs and the consultants suggestions may throw some light on the inadequacies related to the quality. According the respondents consultants as well as their association (IMCI) were asked to comment upon these aspects and the their response has been analised and presented below.

3.1 EMPLOYMENT PATTERN OF FULL TIME CONSULTANTS

All the respondents were asked to indicate the number of consultants employed on full time basis excluding the promoter. The data reported has been analysed and the position is as under.

TABLE 3.1

Employment pattern of full time consultants

S.No.	*No. of consultants per unit*	*No of consultancy firms*	*%*
1	Zero	31	30.00
2	One	15	14.50
3	Two	12	11.50
4	3-5	18	17.50
5	6-10	12	11.50
6	11-20	06	06.00
7	Above 20	09	09.00
	Total	103	100.00

It is evident from the above that 30% of the consultancy firms are solo consultancy firms, 14.50% have only one consultant, 11.50% have two consultants and 17.50% employ between 3 to 5 consultants. Thus majority of the consultancy firms (56%) employ only two or less consultants. 85% of the firms have 10 or less consultants. Thus it may be safely concluded that majority of the firms do not face any organisational complexity. Such small consultancy organisations should be non bureaucratic, informal, facilitate professional development of consultants and should be able to provide environment conductive for professional excellence and good quality consultancy service. Therefore why they are not able to provide consultancy services of reasonable quality as per customer's needs should be probed.

3.2 EMPLOYMENT PATTERN OF PART TIME CONSULTANTS

Apart from obtaining information on full time employment, the consultancy firms were requested to indicate the no. of consultants employed on part time basis. The data so received has been analysed and the position is as under

TABLE 3.2

Employment pattern part time consultants

S.No.	*No. of consultants per firm*	*No. of firms*	*%*
(1)	Zero	38	37.00
(2)	Below 5	47	45.50
(3)	6 -10	11	10.50
(4)	11 -20	03	03.00
(5)	Above 20	04	04.00
	Total	103	100

It is seen that majority of consultancy firms (63%) depend upon part time consultants. However 45.50% firms employ less than 5 consultants on part time basis. Thus it can be concluded that majority of the consultancy firms have part time consultants on their panel and utilise their services whenever need arises. This practice is felt necessary to reduce the overheads and to take care of wide fluctuations in the demand for consultancy services. This also enable them to provide different services under one roof.

3.3 ACADEMIC BACKGROUND OF THE CONSULTANTS

The academic and professional background of the consultants is major factor expected to contribute to the quality of service. The data about academic and professional qualifications was asked jointly for both full time and part time consultants. Analysis of data reveals position shown in table 3.3.

It is evident from the analysis indicated above that 46.50 consultancy firms employ management graduates, 30% Engineers, 32% Engg. with M.B.A, 30% cost/chartered accountants.

TABLE 3.3

Academic background of the consultants

S.No.	*Qualifications*	*Total No. of consultancy firms (out of 103 firms)*	*%*
1	MBA	48	46.50
2	B.Tech./M.Tech	31	30.00
3	Engg. With M.B.A	33	32.00
4	F.C.A./I.C.W.A.	32	30.00
5	M.Com./M.A(Eco.)	04	04.00
6	Other	42	41.00

Data related to academic/professional profile of consultants on roll was given a different treatment. Numbers of consultants having various academic/professional profile with respondent consultancy firms were added to know total number of consultants having these academic/professional profiles and the data so obtained was compared to know the share of consultants having different academic/professional profiles. The analysis of the data reveals the position shown below.

TABLE 3.4

Total number of consultants having different academic/ professional profiles

S.No.	*Qualification*	*No. of consultants*	*Share in %*
1	MBA	159	16.60
2	B.Tech./M.Tech	265	27.60
3	Engg with M.B.A	139	14.50
4	F.C.A/ I.C.W.A	60	06.20
5	M.Com/M.A.(Eco.)	25	02.60
6	other	312	32.50
	Total	960	100.00

It may be seen from the above that majority of the consultants are professionals. However, the technocrats are dominating over the management graduates (42.10% Technocrats in comparison to 31.10% management graduates). This is probably due to dominant use of consultants for project consultancy by the SSI sector but now the management graduates have now become a force to reckon with. The most significant finding is presence of 32.5% i.e. one third are non-professionals. This indicates that consultancy profession has to go a long way so far professionalism is concerned. This may be one of the important bottleneck in providing good quality services. Therefore though the academic/ professional background of the of consultants appears to be quite suitable for providing consultancy services to SSI clients as per their needs but the final comments can be made only after ascertaining their real consultancy needs.

3.4 EXPERIENCE PROFILE OF CONSULTANTS

All the firms were asked to indicate the experience profile of all their consultants whether on full time or part time. Data has been received and analysed and the position is as under.

TABLE 3.5

Experience profile of consultants

S.No.	*Experience in years*	*No. of consultancy firms (out of 103)*	*%*
1	Below 5	23	22.30
2	5-10	43	41.75
3	11-15	50	48.50
4	Above 15	72	70.00

It is seen frcm the above that 70% of the consultancy organisations employ consultants having experience above 15 years.

Data related to experience of consultants on roll was given a different treatment. Numbers of consultants having various lengths of experience with respondent consultancy firms were added to know total number of consultants having these range of experience and the data so obtained was compared to know the share of consultants having different experience profile. The analysis of the data reveals the position shown below.

TABLE 3.6

Total number of consultants having different experience profiles

S.No.	*Length of experience (years)*	*Total No of consultants*	%
1	Below 5	132	13.80
2	5-10	174	18.00
3	11-15	214	22.30
4	Above 15	440	45.90
	Total	960	100.00

It may be seen from the above that majority of the consultants are having experience between 10 years 15 years. Therefore it may be concluded that majority of the consultants have experience of over 10 years but the quality of this experience will depend upon the type of assignments they have done in the past.

3.5 MANAGEMENT PROBLEMS OF SSI UNITS

The IMCI was asked to indicate the major management problems of SSI units and their relative importance. Their response has been analised and presented in table 3.7.

Thus it can be seen that the project conception and implementation stage mistakes have been rated to be the major problem followed by financial problems like use of resource and lack of costing systems, marketing, entrepreneurial inadequacy, lack of systems, bad quality of products and inventory built up in that order.

TABLE 3.7

**Management Problems of SSI units
(As rated by the IMCI)**

Rank	*Management Problem*
I	Pre-production mistakes
II	Optimum use of funds
III	Marketing problems
IV	One man show
V	Problem of system and costing
VI	Training of supervisors and the entrepreneurs
VII	Quality of products
VIII	High inventory built up
IX	Financial problems

3.6 MANAGEMENT CONSULTANCY NEEDS OF SSI UNITS

The consultancy needs as rated by IMCI has been presented below:

TABLE 3.8

**Management consultancy needs of the SSI units
(As rated by the IMCI)**

Rank	*Management Consultancy Needs*
I	Proper project consultancy
II	Help in market development
III	Introduce cost reduction methods
IV	Train the entrepreneur and his staff
V	Enforce quality controls
VI	Study inventory management Systems and suggest improvements

Thus, it may be seen that IMCI perceives project consultation as the most important service followed by market development, financial services like cost reduction and training to the owner and his staff followed by suggestions for quality controls and rationalisation of inventories etc.

3.7 AVAILABLE CONSULTANCY SERVICES

All the respondents consultancy firms were requested to indicate the type of services being offered by them. The data has been analysed and the position is as under

TABLE 3.9

Relative ranking of available consultancy services

S.No.	*Description of service*	*Number of consultancy firms extending service*
	A. Project Management Services	
1	Project consultancy	28
2	Market surveys	25
3	Techno-economic feasibility Reports/ Detailed project Reports	21
4	Turn key projects	18
5	Revival of sick units	09
6	Project identification	08
7	Project appraisal	07
8	NSIC Registration	06
9	Industrial potential surveys	05
10	Merchant banking	02
11	Coordination with Govt. agencies	02
12	Location studies	01
13	Data bank for industries	01
	Total(A)	133

	(B) General management services	
1	Systems and procedures	12
2	Productivity/process studies	11
3	Organisational development studies	09
4	Review of organisational structure	06
5	Corporate planning	06
6	Diagnostic study of sick units	05
7	Profitability improvement studies	05
8	Work/Job studies	05
9	Study of material handling process	04
10	General management studies	04
11	Cost audit/reduction studies	04
12	Management Audit	03
13	Design Management Information System	03
14	General system design and development	02
15	Industrial Engg	02
16	Company formation	02
17	Performance optimisation	01
18	Design standard costing system	01
19	Design support systems	01
20	Develop project controls and monitoring system	01
	Total(B)	87
	(C) Personnel Management Services	
1	Training in management development	49
2	Selections/recruitment	19
3	Peoples opinion surveys	02
4	Manpower Motivation	02
5	Training needs analysis	01
	Total(C)	73

	(D) Production Management Services	
1	Energy conservation	13
2	Modernisation Studies	12
3	Technology Transfer	08
4	Quality Management	05
5	Pollution controls	04
6	Store audit	04
7	Study of plant layout	03
8	Technology survey	03
9	Inventory control systems	03
10	Value Engg	01
11	Technical audit of equipments	01
12	Streamlining preventive maintenance systems	01
	Total (D)	58

	(E) Marketing Management Services	
1	Market identification	12
2	Formulating market development strategies	11
3	Market development	05
4	Export market supports	04
5	Sell product on commission basis	04
6	Market testing of new products	02
7	International alliance strategy for the SSIs	02
8	Marketing Audit	01
9	Administration	01
10	Product pricing and product mix decisions	01
11	Develop dealership systems	01
12	Industrial marketing	01
13	Rural marketing	01
14	Campaign for new products	01
	Total (E)	47

	(F) Financial Management Services	
1	Valuation of assets	13
2	Financial arrangements	10
3	Developing financial management system	04
4	Corporate financial advice	03
5	Install prudent control systems	02
6	Lease finance management	01
7	Bill discounting	01
	Total (F)	34
	(G) Other management services	
1	Management consultancy on retainership basis	06
2	Computeristion	05
3	Management agency system of assistance	03
4	Transport consultancy service	02
5	Legal advice for economic legislation	02
6	Computer crime investigation	01
7	Arbritrations	01
8	Develop internal consultancy capability	01
9	Student guidance	01
10	Town planning	01
11	Construction management	01
	Total(G)	24

3.8 RELATIVE IMPORTANCE OF VARIOUS FUNCTIONAL AREAS

The weightage of the a functional management area has been used to ascertain its relative importance. The position turns out to be as in table 3.10.

It may be seen from the position available above that project consultancy is the major area of consultation followed by general management, personnel, production, marketing,

TABLE 3.10

Relative importance of management consultancy services in various functional areas

S.No.	*Functional area of management*	*Weightage*	*Rank*
1	Project management services	133	I
2	General management services	87	II
3	Personnel management services	73	III
4	Production management services	58	IV
5	Marketing management services	47	V
6	Financial management services	34	VI
7	Other management consultancy services	24	VII

finance and other areas in order of importance. However in these areas the detailed inter say position is as under:

(a) Project management consultancy services

Major project consultancy services in order of their rank or importance are market surveys to ascertain the likely demand of the products proposed to be manufactured, preparation of techno-economic feasibility reports/detailed project reports for new projects, turn key consultancy, revival of sick units, identification of good project ideas, appraisal of project on behalf of financial institutions, assistance in getting the unit registered with National Small Industries Corporation or state directorate of industries and conducting industrial potential surveys to identify industrial potential of a area. It is further seen that the entrepreneurs are going to the consultants for getting loan or some other benefits from any govt. agency.

(b) General management services

Major general management consultancy services being made available in order of importance are review/modification of systems/procedures, productivity studies, organisational development studies, review of organisation structure, diagnosis of sick units, implementation of profit improvement studies, work/ job study. Study of the process, study/review of general management systems, study to reduce cost, management audit and other miscellaneous general management services such as designing management information system, industrial engg., company formation, performance appraisal and design costing system.

(c) Personnel management services

Major personnel services in order of their relative importance are training to the executives and entrepreneurs for developing managerial skills (39%), recruitment/ selections(20%), training to develop the skills in the workers/ supervisors (8%), and other services such as training for quality, people opinion survey, manpower motivation and training need analysis. Thus it may be seen that executive and non-executive training is main pre-occupation of the personnel consultants followed by selection but other areas are not getting adequate attention.

(d) Production management consultancy services

Major areas in order of importance are advising on energy conservation, modernisation study, facilitating technology transfer, quality management. Pollution controls, store audit, study of plant layout, technology surveys, study of inventory control systems, system design for optimisation of purchases, value engg, technical audit of equipments and streamlining preventive maintenance system. So it can be seen that consultancy in production area in mostly centered around systems of different types.

(e) Marketing management consultancy services

Major consultancy services in order of importance are market identification, formulating market development studies, market development, export market supports, selling products on commission basis and test marketing for new products (not exactly a consultancy service as per the definition adopted the researcher), and other misc. marketing services such as advising of international alliance strategy for SSI units, marketing audit, product pricing and mix, dealership development system, industrial marketing rural marketing and compaign for new products. Therefore, the major services are connected with market development.

(f) Financial management consultancy services

Major financial services in order of their importance are valuation of assets, (13%) assisting the client company in arranging finance (10%), review of existing financial management systems or design a new one for the client (4%), corporate financial advice (3%), design and install budget control systems (2%), assist in getting lease finance (15) and bill discounting. Here the main emphasis appears to be on getting finances from all possible sources at minimum possible cost and other issue related to optimal management of this fund are not important to the entrepreneurs.

(g) Other consultancy services

Other major areas of consultation are computerisation, management agency services, legal advice for economic legislation and other services such as arbitration, develop internal consultancy etc. Now the computers are coming in big way and this area has big potential.

3.9 METHODS OF CHARGING CONSULTANCY FEE

All the consultants were requested to indicate the method being followed by them in assessing the consultancy fee. This data has been analised and the position is indicated in table 3.11.

It may be seen from the above that the predominant methods are consultants man days for ongoing units and as a percentage of project cost for new units. The other methods are not popular as yet.

TABLE 3.11

Methods of estimating consultancy charges

S.No.	*Basis of estimation*	*No of consultancy firms*
1	Consultant's man days	73
2	Percentage of project cost	36
3	Lump sum amount	19
4	Percentage of sales	07
5	Percentage of saving	03
6	Other methods	12

3.10 MODE OF ENGAGEMENT

Consultants may be engaged on assignment to assignment basis, or retainership basis or both. All the respondents were asked to indicate the mode of engagement being followed by the clients. The data received from this has been analysed and the results are under.

TABLE 3.12

Mode of engagement

S.No.	*Mode*	*No of consultancy firms*	*%*
1	Assignment basis	59	57
2	Retainership	10	10
3	Both	34	33
	Total	103	100

It is evident from the above that majority of the consultants (90%) are being engaged on assignment basis where the relationship terminates with the completion of the assignment followed by retainership basis (43%) including mix pattern. Normally for the new projects, consultants are engaged for the specific assignment and for consultancy to on going units is on retainership basis where the relations are of long term nature.

3.11 MANAGEMENT CONSULTANCY FIRMS SERVING SSI UNITS

Out of 103 respondents 02 did not indicate whether they serve SSI units or not. However 66 consultants said that they serve SSI units and the remaining 25 replied in negative. Thus the assessment of various dimensions of management consultancy services is based on the experience of these 66 consultancy organisations. Similarly the reasons for not serving the small scale sector is based on the analysis of the response of these 25 consultancy firms.

3.12 SHARE OF SSI UNITS IN THE TOTAL ANNUAL TURNOVER OF THE CONSULTANCY FIRMS

All the respondents were asked to indicate the share of SSIs units in the total annual consultancy turnover. The data received has been analysed and the result is placed below

TABLE 3.13

Annual consultancy turn over- share of SSI sector

S.No.	*Share of SSIs*	*No of consultancy firms*	*%*
1	Below 25%	23	35
2	26%-50%	16	24
3	51%-75%	12	18
4	Above 75%	15	23
	Total	66	100

It may be seen from the above that about 60% of the consultancy firms are having below 50% of the annual consultancy turnover from the SSIs and only 23% firms have over 75% turnover from the SSI sector. It appears that most of the consultants have to depend upon medium and large units for their survival. As such they are not in a position to concentrate on the SSI sector.

3.13 REASONS FOR NOT SERVING SSI UNITS

It has already mentioned that 25 respondents did not serve SSI units. They were asked to state reasons for not serving this sector in order of their importance. The reasons disclosed by them have been analysed and ranked in descending order in the table given below

TABLE 3.14

Reasons for not serving small scale industrial units

Rank	*Reasons*	*No. of firms*
I	Inability of SSIs to bear the cost of service they require	17
II	SSIs are not aware about the importance of management consultancy services	12
III	Consultancy fee is high due to high overheads of large consultancy firms	05
IV	Small firms do not have complicated organisation as such no consultancy required	05
V	SSI units do not implement the recommendations	04
VI	Specialise only for large units	03
VII	SSIs do not know that management consultants exist	02
VIII	SSIs do not know their real needs and are not ready to listen	02
IX	Indirect service	02
X	SSIs are mostly sick due to pre -production mistakes and such nothing can be done	02
XI	SSIs do not know how to use consultants	01
XII	Banks/ govt. agencies do not co-operate with the consultants	01

It is evident from the above that major cause for not serving the SSI is reported to be high cost of service due to high overheads and lack of appreciation of the importance of the management consultancy services by the SSI units coupled with other reasons such as non-implementation of recommendations, lack of expertise needed for SSI units, non- awareness about their real problems as well as existence of management consultants, consultants' inability to solve the problems inherited due to pre production mistakes and inability of the SSI entrepreneurs in ensuring optimal utilisation of management consultants. Therefore according to the consultants high cost of service, lack of awareness about existence of consultants, how to use them and benefits of management consultancy services and lack of expertise for SSI are major reasons for nor serving SSI units. However considering the importance attached by them to the improvement of awareness of SSI entrepreneurs about the benefits of management consultancy services and marketing efforts while suggesting steps for improving the utilisation of management consultancy services during post production period, it appears that they provide greater importance to lack of awareness than cost of services.

However according to IMCI the major reasons utilsing the services of management consultants by SSI units in that order are non-awareness on the part of the entrepreneurs about the utility of management consultants in solving their problems, mistrust of SSI on the consultants with regards to leakage of their trade secrets and the rules they break very often.

Thus it can be concluded that supplier group perceives lack of awareness in the SSI entrepreneurs about the benefits of consultants and their existence, high cost of service and lack of expertise for SSI units to be the major reasons for not serving SSI units. It may also mean that these are the reasons for not availing management consultancy services by the SSI units during post-production period.

3.14 MAJOR PROBLEMS OF CONSULTANTS WHILE DEALING WITH THE SSI UNITS

The consultants who serve SSI units (66 Firms) were further asked to indicate the major problems they normally face with the SSI units while providing consultancy services to them. They were also asked to rank these problems in order of importance.

The data have been analysed and presented below.

TABLE 3.15

Major problems of consultants with the SSI units

Rank	*Problem*	*No. of firms*
I	SSI owners do not understand the importance of management consultancy and therefore they consider the expenditure on consultancy a waste and come only when compelled by some financial institution or govt. agency.	44
II.	They create problems in payment due to poor financial position.	32
III	There is lack of professionalism on the part of the SSI entrepreneurs and such they manage their units in unprofessional manner, do not train their staff and do not attach any importance to managerial inputs.	25
IV	They do not want to pay consultancy fee, want it free and do not realise the viability problems of consultants.	24
V	They do not trust the consultants and as such neither they provide full information to them nor let them talk to their staff.	17
VI	They hesitate to implement our recommendations but blame the consultants for their failures	09
VII	Govt. has discontinued the consultancy fee subsidy scheme and as such the fee has become costly for small units.	08

cont...

VIII	There is total lack of consultancy culture in the country.	07
IX	There is tough competition from unscrupulous elements posing as consultants but working as middle men between the corrupt officials of the financial institutions without any professional ethics.	07
X	Consultancy is not considered preventive but curative and such the SSI units come to consultants when forced by some internal or external trouble that too at the last stage like patients going to doctor at the critical stage. This is typical Indian psyic to postpone the doctor till you can.	05
XI	They do not understand their own management problems and the service which they require.	05
XII	Financial institutions do not want to deal with the consultants directly.	04
XIII	The SSI entrepreneurs do not realise the importance of improving the quality of their products or of acquiring national or international quality certification.	04
XIV	The SSI units which are doing relatively better do not consider the possibility of further improvement.	03
XV	We do not have requisite expertise in the management area for SSI units.	02
XVI	SSI units most of the time mis -interpret the terms and conditions of the consultancy contract and demand more without any payment	02
XVII	They are not ready to grow as they want to remain within the limit set for small scale sector	02
XVIII	We face problems in marketing our services to SSI units.	01
XIX	Lack of continuity in business.	01
XX	SSI units do not provide proper time to complete the job and want quick results.	01

The above table presents the major problems in very clear terms and as such no further elaboration is considered necessary. However these issues were also raised with the user units and their responses have been then compared with the views of the consultants.

3.15 SUGGESTIONS OF THE CONSULTANTS FOR IMPROVING THE PRESENT STATE OF AFFAIRS

All the respondents were requested to suggest the ways and means to improve the use of management consultancy services by the SSI sector. Their suggestions have been analysed and placed below in order of their importance.

TABLE 3.16

Suggestions of the consultants to improve the situation

S.No.	*Suggestion*	*No of consultancy firms*
I	**Develop awareness about importance of management consultancy services in SSI entrepreneurs and remove their mental blocks about the consultants by**	**19**
(i)	Brain storming sessions at the industrial estates jointly by IMCI and Industry Associations	08
(ii)	Seminars/penal discussions by IMCI	07
(iii)	Frequent interactions between the entrepreneurs and the consultants	03
(iv)	Training to the entrepreneurs about the use of consultants	01
(II)	**Consultants should market their services by**	**13**
(i)	They should approach FIs for empenelment and for the circulation of the penel amongst the branches of these institutions. Similarly they could approach industry associations industrial development authorities, state directorate of industries and DICs etc.	06
(ii)	The consultants should approach professionally qualified SSI entrepreneurs, work for them and then try to get references from them. However for this they have to demonstrate that benefits from their consultancy will be more than the cost of service.	04
(iii)	They should develop long term rapport with the SSI units through retainer consultancy.	02

cont...

(iv)	They may try appointments at the board level.	01
III	**Following steps may be taken to reduce the cost of consultancy for the SSI units to bring it down to their payment capacity**	**08**
(i)	Govt. should subsidise /finance consultancy fee	03
(ii)	The consultants may serve 5 or 6 SSI units on retainership basis charging Rs 2000 to Rs 3000 per month depending upon the payment capacity.	02
(iii)	The initial consultancy fee can be shared by the user unit Industry associations and the DICs and subsequently 10% of the productivity gain can go to the consultants and 30 % to the association and DIC.	02
(iv)	Solo consultants with no office overheads working on retainership basis may become affordable by the SSI units	01
(v)	Retired persons having suitable industry and managerial experience may work for SSI units on retainership basis.	01
IV	**Promoters' commitment to the growth of the SSI units could be improved through following steps**	**03**
(i)	Increase margin money requirement from 15% to 35%	01
(ii)	Turn -over incentives to the SSI entrepreneurs	01
(iii)	Govt. agencies should not run after the entrepreneurs	01
V	**Quality of consultancy services could be improved by taking following steps**	**03**
(i)	Thorough training of consultants by the IMCI	02
(ii)	By gaining practical experience	01
VI	**To improve the understanding between the SSI entrepreneurs and the consultants following steps can be taken**	**02**
(i)	The scope for the consultancy should be clearly defined even in case of retainership	01
(ii)	Clear understanding about the consultancy contract	01
VII	**The DICs and the TCOs should strengthen themselves in the area of management consultancy requirements of the small scale sectors with the support of their sponsoring institutions**	**01**

The suggestions given by the consultancy firms and ranked above do not require any further clarification except than comparing them with the suggestions of the user group and the FIs.

According to the IMCI following actions may improve the utilisation of management consultancy services by SSI units.

(i) The management consultancy services should be made compulsory like the audit by CAs for the limited companies, cooperative societies and charities.

(ii) Members of IMCI may be deputed to various industry associations for increasing the awareness of the SSIs about the benefits of management consultancy services. Also industry associations may be persuaded to organise meetings of their members with the consultants.

(iii) It may prepare a list of consultants who are ready to serve SSI units and then circulate the list to all the associations for use.

It seen that the whole emphasis of IMCI is on making the service compulsory and then creating awareness and no emphasis has been is laid on improving the quality of service.

Thus, it may be concluded that the suppliers group feels that developing awareness about importance of management consultancy services for SSI units, marketing of the services, reducing the cost of services, improving commitment of the SSI entrepreneurs in the growth of their units,. improving the quality of consultancy service, and understanding their real management problems can improve the utilisation of management consultancy services by SSI units during the post production period.

3.16 THE QUALITY CONTROL MECHANISM OF INSTITUTE OF MANAGEMENT CONSULTANTS OF INDIA(IMCI)

The IMCI aims at ensuring that the profession of management consultancy is recognised, respected and accepted as providing a valuable service to all category of organisations in industry, trade, commerce, govt. public and other services. This research aims at studying the quality dimensions of management consultancy services to SSI units. The SSI sector requires a particular type of service and how far the existing management consultants are able to give satisfactory services to it is the issue under investigation. So far it appears that bad quality services coupled with high costs of service and lack of urge in SSIs to professionalise are basic reasons for low use of management consultancy services by the SSI units. Thus it is seen the IMCI has failed to maintain the standard of service of its members to the SSI sector. If we study the reason of this failure the following reasons are clearly visible.

(I) The institute has around 300 members only out of about 15000 consultants reportedly working in India. So it's impact is hardly visible.

(II) Most of its members serve only large units and are hardly interested in serving Small sector. Therefore IMCI does not take any active interest in developing management consultancy for SSI units.

(III) There is no provision for professional qualifications for becoming member of the institute and only the word suitable qualification has been mentioned in the bylaws.

(IV) There is no provision for compulsory written or viva voice test before a person can be admitted as affiliate member or his category changed to member or fellow.

(V) There is no visible efforts on the part of IMCI to enhance the professional standard of its members except for holding some seminars etc.

In view of the above it will be better to establish separate institute for consultants serving small units.

4

Perception of the Customer Group—Small Scale Industrial Units and their Associations

The quality of consultancy services has direct correlation with the types of services being provided vis-à-vis actual consultancy needs of the customers depending upon the extent of employment of management degree/diploma holders by them and their satisfaction level. Further as high lighted in the literature survey quality depends upon personal competence of the consultant, effectiveness of the selection procedure, extent of use by the client, cost of service, consultant's style, implementation strategies, quality control mechanism and general environmental factors. It is also essential to review other general aspects such as functions, area of consultancy and problems being faced by both the consultants and the clients. According while interviewing SSI units, their response was obtained on relevant aspects such as extent of employment of management degree/diploma holders, level of satisfaction with the current level of performance, perception about the role of professional management practices in solving internal and external problems, internal management problems, real consultancy needs, extent of utilisation of consultancy services, reasons for not using consultants both in the pre production and post production periods; sector of consultants used, types of services availed, consultancy fee paid, time taken in completing the assignment, implementation of the recommendations, satisfaction level with the services availed in the past, major deficiencies in services, methods used to diagnose the problems, method employed in choosing consultants, actual benefits vis-à-vis initial expectations from the consultant, quality of consultancy contract, problems faced while availing consultancy services, possibility of repeat hiring of the consultant used in the past, perception about the ability of management consultants in improving the efficiency of SSIs, payment capacity of SSIs, mode of engagement and suggestions for improving the utilisation of consultancy services by the SSI units. Therefore data and views of the members of the user group i.e. SSI units and their associations (7 nos.) has been collected and analysed and the results are presented below.

4.1 EMPLOYMENT OF MANAGEMENT DEGREE/ DIPLOMA HOLDERS BY SSI UNITS

Out of the 50 respondents who replied to this question, only 9 employed M.B.A. (18%) and the remaining 82% of the units did not employed them at all. We have already seen that only 10% of the entrepreneurs have management degree even when the sample is biased in favour of bigger and relatively well organised urban units. Those who employ M.B.A normally employ one or two persons having managerial expertise and they have experience below 10 years.

While interviewing the industry associations the researcher tried to find out the general profile of the SSI units. The secretary of the Vadodara chamber of commerce and industry informed that 90% of the units of Makarpura industrial estate employed less than 20 workers, only 10% entrepreneurs were technical graduates/post graduates, 5% M.B.As and the rest were nonprofessionals. Most of the units were very small having investment below 10 lakhs and sales below 20 lakhs. This is position of the SSI units located in the industrial estate of Vadodara, a high growth industrial township of western India. Considering the fact that majority of the SSI are located in smaller towns and rural areas, it may be said that most of the SSI units are very small and the entrepreneurs have lower qualifications. However its felt that with increase in professionalisation the demand for management consultants is likely to increase. The manufacturing associations are also providing consultancy just to sell their machines but they are providing technical consultancy and not management consultancy. Most of the associations are of the view that the consultants should be first engaged on assignment basis and then on retainer basis for solving post-production problems.

Therefore question of employing management degree/ diploma holders in such remote and ill equipped places does not arise. Therefore it may be concluded that Small scale sector does not has any worthwhile in-house managerial expertise except the management background of very few entrepreneurs and as such it should normally depend upon external help to solve its management/other problems.

4.2 SATISFACTION FROM THE PRESENT LEVEL OF PERFORMANCE

All the respondents were asked to state whether they are satisfied with the current level of performance. Only 27.45% replied in affirmative whereas remaining 72.55% units were not satisfied. Thus it can be concluded that about three fourth of the SSI units are not functioning well. This has been also confirmed by several studies referred in the literature research. Thus this fact gets validated. As such there should be high demand for management consultancy services from the SSIs as majority of them are not performing well and are not satisfied.

4.3 PERCEPTION ABOUT ROLE OF PROFESSIONAL MANAGEMENT PRACTICES IN SOLVING THE MANAGEMENT PROBLEMS

Respondents were asked whether they believed that good

management practices can solve management problems of small scale sector. In response 45 out of 51 respondents (88.22%) replied in affirmative. Thus it can be said that at least the professionally qualified entrepreneurs have high faith in the usefulness of management tools and techniques. It is a fact that the sample is heavily biased towards well qualified entrepreneurs and as such the share of small unit owners having positive attitude towards modern management tools may come down if the sample also includes rural and semi-urban entrepreneurs running relatively smaller units than those being represented by this sample. However it may be safely concluded that with rising educational levels and fast changing technology the relative share of such enlightened entrepreneurs is likely to increase in future and as such the prospects of management consultants is likely to be bright and it should be categorised as sun rise industry.

4.4 MANAGEMENT PROBLEMS OF SSI UNITS—THE RANK ANALYSIS

All the respondents were requested to indicate the major internal management problems in order of their importance. The problems indicated by them have been analysed taking into account the rank assigned to them. The result of analysis is as under

(i) First rank

(a) Marketing management problems were assigned first rank by 26 units (51%). Out of 26 units, 15 units had general marketing problems, 6 units were facing the problems of new markets and remaining 5 units were facing tough competition. Thus pushing product in the market in face of a growing competition is the major concern of the small units.

(b) Financial management problems were reported as number one problem by 19 units. Out of 19 units 11 units reported working capital problems, 4 units optimal use of funds, 2 units poor collection of funds, 1 unit lack of financial plans and one unit delay in getting loan. It may be seen that most of the respondents feel that inadequacy of funds to be major problem than the optimisation of whatever funds they may have. This perception was also reported by Harper Malcolm(84) and many official studies reported in the literature research. Therefore the said perceptions of the entrepreneurs get confirmed by this study.

(c) Personnel management problems were reported by 7 units as first ranking problems. The major personnel problems were negative attitudes of the staff and supervisors (2 units), labor trouble (2Units), non-availability of technically competent manpower and fast turnover of employees coupled with the lack of managerial skills in the entrepreneurs. It can be seen that it is the manpower productivity which is major problem and how to get best from them is concern of most of the small units where the output mostly depends upon the manpower.

(d) Production related management problems were ranked first by only two units who complained about various production problems .

(ii) Second Rank

(1) Financial management problems were ranked second by 16 units, the major financial problems being financial problems (6units), proper use of funds (5units), problems in repayment of loans i.e. profitability/liquidity problems (4units) and use of funds (2units).

(2) Marketing management problems were ranked second by 12 units, the major marketing problems being general marketing problems (5units), market survey (4units) market exploration for new product (2units) and advertising (1unit). It is thus seen that to push the product in the market is the major concern of these units.

(3) Personnel management problems were ranked second

by 7 units, major problems being labor problems (4units), non- availability of the technical manpower (1unit), poor attendance (1unit) and unreasonable labor demand (1unit). Therefore the main problem is how to take full benefits from the labour.

(4) Production management problems were ranked second by 7 units, major problems being production scheduling (2units), problem of raw materials (2units), technical problems (2units) and purchase/ inventory problems(1unit). Thus production problems are more concerned with ensuring timely output.

(5) General management problems were ranked second by only 3 units, problems being lack of data on demand, lack of periodicals for SSI sector and instability of the system each reported by one unit.

(iii) Third Rank

(I) **Personnel management problems** were ranked 3rd by 13 units, labour trouble being the major problem (8units).

(II) **Production management problems** were reported 3rd by 6 units major problem being that of quality (5 units).

(III) **Working capital problem** were reported third by 5 units.

(IV) **Project management problems** were reported third by 2units the problems being poor coordination with the govt. agencies and confusions in the duties of the partners about their role in the implementation of the project.

(V) **General management problem** was ranked third by one unit who said that the SSI entrepreneurs do not have clear perception about real problems of their units.

(iv) Fourth Rank

(I) Financial management problems were ranked fourth

by 4 units , main problem being working capital (2units) and general problems.

(II) Personnel management problems were ranked fourth by only 2 units problems being unsatisfactory supervisory capability and non availability of competent manpower. They are not talking of training their staff.

(III) Production management problems were ranked fourth by 2 units, the problems being raw materials.

(IV) Marketing management problems were ranked fourth by only one units which was bothered about sales problem.

If we consider only the number of units giving first rank to a functional area of management and rank the functional areas on this basis, it is seen that marketing management is main problem (26 units) followed by finance (19 units), personnel (7 units) and production (2 units). However we may ascertain the relative ranks of various functional areas of management by assigning following marks to various ranks and then finding out cumulative weighted marks for various functional areas..

TABLE 4.1

Weight of various ranks

Rank	*Weighted Mark*
I	4
II	3
III	2
IV	1

Taking into account the number of units giving a particular rank the weighted cumulative marks of each functional area of management can be as under-

TABLE 4.2

Cumulative weighted marks of marketing management problems

Rank	*No. of units assigning rank*	*Cumulative marks*
I	26	104
II	12	36
III	0	0
IV	1	1
	Total	141

TABLE 4.3

Cumulative weighted marks of financial management problems

Rank	*No. of units assigning rank*	*Cumulative marks*
I	19	76
II	16	48
III	5	10
IV	4	4
	Total	138

TABLE 4.4

Cumulative weighted marks of personnel management problems

Rank	*No. of units assigning rank*	*Cumulative marks*
I	7	28
II	7	21
III	13	26
IV	2	02
	Total	77

TABLE 4.5

Cumulative weighted marks of production management problems

Rank	*No. of units assigning rank*	*Cumulative marks*
I	2	8
II	7	21
III	6	12
IV	2	2
	Total	43

TABLE 4.6

Cumulative weighted marks of project management problems

Rank	*No. of units assigning rank*	*Cumulative marks*
I	0	0
II	0	0
III	2	4
IV	0	0
	Total	4

TABLE 4.7

The relative cumulative weighted marks of various management problems

Functional area of mgt.	*Cumulative weighted marks*	*Rank*
Marketing mgt.	141	I
Financial mgt.	138	II
Personnel mgt.	77	III
Production mgt.	43	IV
Project mgt.	4	V

Thus, it may be concluded that as per the SSI respondents marketing and financial management problems are main areas of concern for the SSI units followed by personnel, production and project management in that order respectively. However the SSI associations identify and rate internal management problems as under.

TABLE 4.8

Management problems of SSI units

S.N.	*Internal Management Problem*	*No. of Associations*	*%*
1	Low demand for the products	06	85.70
2	Lack of control system to ensure optimal use of resources	05	71.43
3	Working capital problem	04	57.14
4	Labour problems	04	57.14
5	Entrepreneurial inadequacies such as lack of marketing skills in the technocrats, lack of integrity/ diversion of funds and ignorance about their real problems.	03	42.29
6	Lack of product scheduling	02	28.57
7	Pre-production mistakes including Selection of wrong machines	02	28.57
8	Non adjustment with changing market conditions	01	14.29
9	Bad quality	01	14.29

From the above, its seen that industry associations also perceive marketing and resource utilisation as the key problem areas of SSI units followed by working capital, labour problems, entrepreneurial inadequacies and pre-production mistakes in that order.

Thus it may be concluded that user group considers marketing and financial management problems as main areas of concern for the SSI units followed by personnel, production and project management in that order respectively.

4.5 MANAGEMENT CONSULTANCY NEEDS OF SSI UNITS

All the respondents were requested to indicate areas of

management in which they normally require consultancy. Their responses have been analysed and the presented rank wise.

TABLE 4.9

Rank analysis of major consultancy needs of SSI units

Rank of		*Area of Management*	*Total No units*
1		2	3
		FIRST RANK	
I. Marketing Management			**33**
	(i)	Guidance for sales promotion	14
	(ii)	Develop market development strategy for competitive markets	09
	(iii)	General marketing	04
	(iv)	Conduct marketing practices surveys	02
	(v)	Market analysis	02
	(vi)	Suggest pricing strategy	01
	(vii)	Export marketing	01
II. Financial management			**16**
	(i)	Assist in getting financial helps	08
	(ii)	Cost reduction	03
	(iii)	General financial management	02
	(iv)	Optimum use of funds	02
	(v)	Financial analysis	01
III. Personnel management			**04**
	(i)	HRD	01
	(ii)	General services	01
	(iii)	Training for the supervisors	01
	(iv)	Training for the entrepreneurs	01
IV. General management			**02**
	(i)	Remove bottlenecks in resource utilisation	01
	(ii)	System development	01

cont...

1	2	3
	SECOND RANK	
I. Financial management		**23**
(i)	Uses of funds / resources	08
(ii)	Arranging loans	06
(iii)	General financial management	03
(iv)	Working capital help	03
(v)	Study of inventory controls system	01
(vi)	Optimisation of purchase cost	01
(vii)	Cost reduction	01
II. Marketing management		**13**
(i)	Market development studies	05
(ii)	Market identification	04
(iii)	Market analysis	03
(iv)	Develop distribution channels	01
III. Production management		**05**
(i)	Study of productivity	01
(ii)	Survey of material	01
(iii)	Inventory controls	01
(iv)	Material optimisation	01
(v)	Quality controls	01
III. General management		**03**
(i)	Resource utilisation	03
	THIRD RANK	
I. Financial management		**11**
(i)	Working capital management	05
(ii)	Use of funds	02
(iii)	Cost analysis and cost reduction	03
(iv)	Introduce cost planning and collection and payment system	01
II. Personnel management		**08**
(i)	Labour problems	03
(ii)	Incentive wages	02
(iii)	HRD	01

cont...

(iv)	Training for the supervisors	01
(v)	Training for motivation	01
III. Production management		**04**
(i)	Waste reduction	02
(ii)	Inventory control	01
(iii)	Technology Upgradation	01
IV. Marketing management		**01**
(i)	Marketing bottlenecks	01
	FOURTH RANK	
I. Financial management		
(i)	Cost reduction	02
(ii)	Financial controls	01
(iii)	Working capital requirements	01
(iv)	Use of funds	01
II. Production management		**01**
(i)	Technology Upgradation	01

If we consider only the number of units giving first rank to the consultancy needs belonging to a functional area of management and rank the functional areas on this basis, it is seen that marketing management consultancy is main consultancy need (33 units) followed by finance (16 units), personnel (4 units) and general management (2 units). However, relative ranks of various management needs of the SSIs, can be also ascertained by assigning following marks to various ranks and the finding out cumulative marks.

TABLE 4.10

Weight of various ranks of consultancy needs

Rank	*Weighted Mark*
I	4
II	3
III	2
IV	1

Taking into account the number of units giving a particular rank the weighted cumulative marks of each functional area of management can be as under-

TABLE 4.11

Cumulative weighted marks of marketing management consultancy needs

Rank	*No. of units assigning rank*	*Cumulative marks*
I	33	132
II	13	39
III	1	2
IV	0	0
	Total	173

TABLE 4.12

Cumulative weighted marks of financial management consultancy needs

Rank	*No. of units assigning rank*	*Cumulative marks*
I	16	64
II	23	69
III	11	22
IV	5	5
	Total	160

TABLE 4.13

Cumulative weighted marks of personnel management consultancy needs

Rank	*No. of units assigning rank*	*Cumulative marks*
I	4	16
II	0	0
III	8	16
IV	0	0
	Total	32

TABLE 4.14

Cumulative weighted marks of production management consultancy needs

Rank	*No. of units assigning rank*	*Cumulative marks*
I	0	0
II	5	15
III	4	8
IV	1	1
	Total	24

TABLE 4.15

Cumulative weighted marks of general management consultancy needs

Rank	*No. of units assigning rank*	*Cumulative marks*
I	2	8
II	3	9
III	0	0
IV	0	0
	Total	17

TABLE 4.16

The relative cumulative weighted marks of various management consultancy needs

Functional area of mgt.	*Cumulative weighted marks*	*Rank*
Marketing mgt.	173	I
Financial mgt.	160	II
Personnel mgt.	32	III
Production mgt.	24	IV
General mgt.	17	V

Thus, we may conclude that SSIs require consultancy services in the areas of marketing, finance, personnel, production and general management in that order of preference. However SSI Associations have rated the consultancy needs of SSI units as under

TABLE 4.17

Management consultancy needs of SSI units (Rated by industry associations)

Rank	*Consultancy needs*	*No of associations*	*%*
I	Help in marketing/sales improvements	05	71.43
II	Optimum use of resources and cost reduction including productivity studies	05	71.43
III	Assist in getting finance	03	42.29
IV	Suggest simple system of control for small units	02	28.57
V	Train the entrepreneurs and his subordinates	02	28.57

It may be seen from the above that as per the perception of the industry associations, development of market/sales, proper use of resources including cost reduction/productivity studies are major consultancy needs followed by arranging finance, suggesting simple control systems and training the entrepreneurs and their subordinates. Thus we may conclude that the user group perceive marketing, finance, personnel, production and general management as major areas of consultation in that order of preference.

(iv) We may total the number of units who have indicated the need for a particular type of service irrespective of the rank assigned to it and then the various consultancy needs may be arranged in descending order irrespective of the functional area to which they belong . If we do in this fashion then the relative importance of first ten management consultancy needs appears to be as under.

TABLE 4.18

Relative importance of consultancy needs of SSI units

Rank	*Consultancy needs*	*No of units*
(i)	Suggest marketing development plan including sales promotion	21
(ii)	Assist in getting financial loans (long and short term)	18
(iii)	Optimise use of funds	17
(iv)	Analysis and reduction of cost	09
(v)	HRD including training to all categories of staff (entrepreneur also)	06
(vi)	Market analysis	05
(vii)	Working capital management	05
(viii)	General financial management	05
(ix)	Market identification	04

It is seen that marketing, finance and personnel are three most important areas.

4.6 UTILISATION OF CONSULTANCY SERVICES BY SSI UNITS

Out of the 51 respondents approached by the researcher only 30(60%) units have utilised the services of consultants in the past. Therefore, the feed back about the quality of service and other relevant aspects is based on the response of these units. Since the sampled units are located in big cities where the consultants are also available, the actual usage of consultants is likely to be very low in rural and semi urban areas where consultants are not available. Therefore, it may be concluded that the use of consultants is very poor. This confirms the findings of literature survey.

4.7 SECTOR OF THE CONSULTANTS ENGAGED

Out of the 30 consultants 25 were from the private sector, 2 from the public sector and remaining two from the Govt. sector. Thus, it can be concluded that private consultants are dominating the scene.

4.8 TYPES OF SERVICES AVAILED

Out of the 30 units 23 units(75%) availed project consultancy services, 3 units marketing management services, 3 units personnel management services and only one unit financial services. However in project management services 17 units got techno-economic feasibility report prepared for loans only, 2 took help in filling the loan application that too for loan, design and development of product for 3 units, and project profile for one unit. Under the marketing management services market networking, policy formulation for sales and export documentation are the services availed. Personnel services consist of only training. Though the arrangement of loans and cost reduction are the main services required by the SSI sector, the emphasis was on getting funds from the market and none of the unit went for cost reduction. Under the general management services formation of company and computerisation were the main services. Thus it could be concluded that utilisation of service is very poor especially for improving internal efficiency. Mostly the services are availed for obtaining some external assistance.

4.9 CONSULTANCY FEE PAID

The data about fee paid has been analysed and the position is as in table 4.19.

Thus it may be seen that over 60% of the user units paid lump sum even for project consultancy work. The consultation charges per consultant per day varies widely between Rs 250 and Rs 5000 depending upon the quality of the consultant and the payment capacity of the unit. Retainer consultation is very uncommon.

TABLE 4.19

Analysis of consultancy fee paid by the user SSI units

Rank	*Basis of charging fee*	*No of units*
I	Lump sum Fee(RS)	*17*
(I)	Below 5000	11
(ii)	5001-10000	02
(iii)	10001-25000	03
(iv)	25001-50000	00
(v)	50001-100000	01
(vi)	Above 100000	00
II	Daily man days rate(in RS)	*03*
(i)	Below 250	01
(ii)	251-500	00
(iii)	501-1000	00
(iv)	1001-5000	00
(v)	Above 5000	02
III	Retainership charges per month (Rs. 10000 per month)	02
IV	As % 0f project cost	01
V	As % of loan amount	01
VI	Free from the govt. consultants	02
VII	Free due to friendship	01
	Total	27

4.10. TIME TAKEN FOR COMPLETING THE ASSIGNMENTS

The respondents were requested to indicate the time taken for completing the assignment. The data received has been analysed and presented below.

TABLE 4.20

Time taken for completing the assignment

S.No.	*Time taken*	*No of units*
(1)	Less than one week	06
(2)	Above one week and up to two weeks	01
(3)	Above two weeks and up to four weeks	10
(4)	Above four weeks and up to three months	06
(5)	Above three months	04
	Total	27

It is clear from the above that in over 60% of the cases the consultants took less that one months time and in 25% cases less than 15 days. Therefore time taken is not major quality problem.

4.11 IMPLEMENTATION OF RECOMMENDATIONS

It is seen that out of 30 units in 9 cases implementation was not required but out of the remaining 21 units 14 implemented and 7 did not implement the recommendations. Thus, it may be said that in 33% cases the recommendations were not implemented. The reasons stated for non implementation was impracticability of the suggestions offered by consultants.

4.12 LEVEL OF SATISFACTION OF THE SSI UNITS

All the respondents were asked to state their level of satisfaction in terms of percentage. The data has been analysed and results are as in table 4.21.

It may be seen from the above that about 63% of the units had satisfaction level below 50% and only 11.00% units were having satisfaction level of 75% and above. Thus it can be concluded that majority of the units are not satisfied from the quality of consultancy services availed by them in the past. In response to a general question about the satisfaction with the consultancy services availed in the past 47% replied in affirmative and the remaining 53% in negative. Thus it can be concluded that majority of the users are not satisfied with the services and such the quality of service was not found to be satisfactory.

TABLE 4.21

Level of satisfaction of SSI units from the consultancy services availed in the past

S.No.	*Level of satisfaction*	*No of units*	*%*
1	Below 25%	05	18.50
2	Above 25%-50%	12	44.50
3	Above 50%-75%	07	25.90
4	Above 75%	03	11.10
	Total	27	100

4.13 METHODS USED TO DETECT THE PROBLEMS BY THE SSI UNITS

The respondents were asked to state as how they came to know about the problems they wanted to solve with the help of the consultants. Their responses have been analysed and the results are placed below.

TABLE 4.22

Method used by SSI units to detect their problems

S.No.	*Methods used*	*No of units*	*% (out of 30)* *% (out of 23)*
1	2	3	4
1	Unit was to be established	13	43.00 (56)
2	Facing cash shortage	03	10.00 (13)
3	Friends indicated the problems	02	06.80 (7.40)
4	Sales were not picking up and was facing export problems	02	06.80 (7.40)

cont...

1	2	3	4
5	Management problems due to increase in size	01	03.35 (4.34)
6	Company was to be formed	01	03.35 (4.34)
7	Taxation problems by the unit	01	03.35 (4.34)
8	Can not say	07	23.35
	Total	30	100.00

It may be seen that in 23% of the units could not reply to this question which means that the engagement of consultants was done on adhoc basis. In 65% cases it did not require any analysis as it was well known and out of compulsion. Out the remaining 8 cases in 2 (8.70%) cases the problems were identified by the friends and only in 3 cases the symptoms were visible because of cash crunch (13%), slow growth in exports (8.70%) and problems due to increase in size (4.34%). Thus it can be concluded that in most of the cases no proper diagnostic/systematic study was done by the user units. This may be one of the reason for low utilisation of services.

4.14 METHODS OF CHOOSING CONSULTANTS

All the respondents were asked to state the methods employed to select a particular consultant. The response has been analysed and the result is placed below.

TABLE 4.23

Methods employed to select consultants

S.No.	*Method used*	*No of units*	%
1	Through friends/relatives	12	42.85
2	Due to reference of govt./FIs	06	21.45
3	Due to audit relationships	05	17.85
4	Self selection	05	17.85
	Total	28	100.00

Thus it may be seen that in over 60% cases the selection was on the basis of previous relations, in 21% cases due to third party intervention and only in 17.85 cases the entrepreneurs selected on their own. Thus past references work out to be prime way to select the consultants followed by on the consideration of third parties. Therefore the process of selection was mostly unscientific and as such selection of good consultants may not be feasible.

4.15 INITIAL EXPECTATIONS OF THE SSI CLIENTS FROM THE CONSULTANTS

The initial expectations as reported by the user SSI units have been analysed and the results are as under.

TABLE 4.24

Original expectations of the SSI units from the consultants

S.No.	*Original expectations*	*No of units*	*%*
1	To get term loan for establishing an unit afresh and then get it established	21	75.0
2	Improve the efficiency	02	07.25
3	For increase in sales	02	07.25
4	To improve the quality of products	01	03.50
5	To get converted into a Pvt. Ltd. company	01	03.50
6	To solve taxation problems	01	03.50
	Total	28	100.00

It is seen that over 75% of the units wanted quick loans of specific amounts from the term lending institutions and banks, 7% of the units to change the constitution or overcome some tax problems. Only 18% units wanted to improve the efficiency, quality and sales. Thus it may be concluded that the intentions to professionalise is hardly present in the SSI entrepreneurs. Therefore they do not go for consultancy services. Once the latent urge to excel is activated in the SSI entrepreneurs, the demand for management consultancy may grow very fast.

4.16 STATEMENT OF INITIAL EXPECTATIONS BY THE CLIENTS

If the initial expectation is clearly stated by the client in the beginning of the assignment, then the consultant can plan and proceed accordingly and it helps him in giving best possible service. However out of the 30 user units only 16 clients specified their expectations clearly to the consultants and in 13 cases it was not spelled out clearly. One unit did not replied to the question. Thus it is seen that over 40% of the units did not specify their expectations. Thus this may be also one of the reasons for poor quality and resultant dissatisfaction.

4.17 EXISTENCE OF CONSULTANCY CONTRACT

For smooth client consultant relations consultancy contract should be entered in to by both the parties. However out of the 30 cases only a appointment letter was issued by the client, in 6 cases and in 22 cases there was nothing. 2 units did not reply to this question. Thus it is seen that in over 70% cases there was no written contract at all. This is likely to lead to mis-understanding between the client and the consultant, which in turn will have adverse effect on the quality of work. Therefore lack of role clarity may be cause of dissatisfaction of the clients at the later stage.

4.18 CLARITY OF TERMS AND CONDITIONS OF CONSULTANCY CONTRACT

For quality service and good understanding between the entrepreneurs and the consultants clarity of terms and conditions is very essential. However out of the 30 user units only 6 units i.e. 20% replied in affirmative and the 22 units i.e. over 70 % said that terms and conditions of the contract were not clear. Remaining 2 unit did not reply to this question. Thus it can be concluded that lack of clarity in most of the cases is major cause of misunderstandings between the clients and the consultants. This may be one of the cause of poor quality of work.

4.19 MAJOR SHORTCOMINGS IN THE CONSULTANCY SERVICES

The respondent SSI units were asked to identify major shortcomings in the services of the consultants. The data received has been analysed and the results are given below.

1. The entrepreneurs had to supply all the technical and market data to the consultants (5 units).
2. The project estimates prepared by the consultants were highly theoretical (4units).
3. The consultants failed to convince the bankers who hardly accepted their recommendations (4 units).
4. Bureaucratic approach by the Govt. consultants (3 units).
5. Training programme arranged by the consultants failed to give practical inputs and proper attention to the each trainee (2 units).
6. Delays in completing the assignment (2 units).
7. Chartered accountants had hardly any experience in the area of management (1 unit).
8. Not available when required (1 unit).
9. No difficulty (7 units).

Therefore it may be seen that quality of service was found to be poor by majority of the units.

4.20 ACTUAL BENEFITS FROM THE CONSULTANCY SERVICES

All the user SSI units were asked to state the benefits

which accrued to them from the consultancy assignment. Analysis of their response indicate that 20 out of 25 units (80%) went for project consultancy and they got the benefits likes loans, formation of the company and setting up of the plant. Out of the remaining 5 units 2 units did not get any benefits, sales increased in 2 cases and marginal improvement in the third case. Therefore dissatisfaction is more acute in regard to the expectation of improved internal efficiency than loans etc.

4.21 PROBLEMS FACED BY THE SSI UNITS WHILE AVAILING THE CONSULTANCY SERVICES

Only 24 user respondents replied to this question and 20 units did not report any problem. Out of the remaining 4 units, 2 units complained of bureaucratic approach of govt. consultants like TCOs and SSIs, one unit said that the unit became sick due to impractical suggestions and remaining one unit complained about the delays in completing the assignment. Thus indirectly the SSI units are complaining about the quality of the service which consists of timely completion of the assignments and offering practical suggestions.

4.22 REPEAT HIRE OF THE OLD CONSULTANTS

One of the measure of the satisfaction is the willingness on the part of clients to repeat the same consultant next time. As such all the respondents who had engaged consultants, were asked to state whether they will like to repeat the same consultant if need arises. In response 12 units out of 30 who replied (38%) replied in affirmative and 18 in negative. Thus it can be said that majority of the user SSI units are not satisfied with the quality of service provided by the consultants as such did not wish to repeat them again.

4.23 ABILITY OF THE MANAGEMENT CONSULTANTS IN IMPROVING THE EFFICIENCY OF THE SSI UNITS

All the respondent SSI units were asked to state whether

they believed that management consultants can improve their efficiency. In response 46 units out of 51 (90%) replied in affirmative and the remaining units in negative. Thus it may be concluded that SSI sector believes in the ability of the management consultants. This is positive indicator of bright future of consultancy profession in India like developed economies.

4.24 PAYMENT CAPACITY OF THE SSI UNITS

Though the payment capacity mostly depends upon the financial conditions of the firm. The researcher made an attempt to explore this area. All the respondents were asked to state the amount they could commit for consultancy. Out of 51 units,14 were not ready to give any estimate, 7units said it depends upon the job and the likely benefits. Out of the remaining 30 units 25 units (83%) were in favour of lump sum amount depending upon the payment capacity of the unit, 4 units (13%) were of the view that it could be as % of sales, 1unit wanted to pay as % of profit. Out of the units who were in favour of paying lump sum, majority of the units (16 units) were ready to pay up to Rs 25000 per annum i.e. Rs 2000 per month approximately followed by 5 units who were ready to pay between above 25000 and below 50000 i.e. Rs 4000 per month 3 units above 50000 and below 100000 and one unit above 100000 i.e. Rs 8000 per month. Since majority of the SSI units are smaller in size and have low payment capacity we may assume a minimum monthly payment capacity of Rs 2000. Out of the 4 units in favour of fee as % of sales 2 units said they can pay up to 0.50% of the sales, 1 unit up to 2% and 1 unit above 2% of the annual sales. Since majority of the SSI units are small size having sales turnover around 5 lakhs, the maximum amount may come around Rs 10000. The unit which favoured fee as % of profit said they can pay up to 5% of the profit. However to have a minimum annual payment of 24000 the unit should have profit of Rs 5 lakhs which is only possible for larger size

SSIs. Thus the % method hardly gives any reliable estimate. It may be said that entrepreneurs should be ready to pay an amount which is at least equal to monthly payment being made to a skilled grade worker. This may not be less than Rs 2000 per month. Therefore monthly retainership charges of Rs 2000 are quite reasonable and may become a guiding factor for the consultants planning their business on retainership basis.

4.25 LEVEL OF EXPECTATIONS OF SSI UNITS FROM THE CONSULTANTS

All the respondent consultants were sure that for minimum satisfaction the benefits from the consultancy assignment should be double than the cost of consultancy. If it can be assured by the consultant then they would be quite ready to engage them.

4.26 MODE OF ENGAGEMENT

All the respondents were asked to state the preferred mode of engagement. Majority of them(52.90%) were in favour of retainership followed by assignment basis (35.30%) and mixed method (On assignment basis for project consultancy and retainership for post production period phase). Thus it can be concluded that retainership is the most preferred mode for engaging consultants during post commissioning period and the assignment basis for project consultancy.

4.27 REASONS FOR NOT UTILISING THE SERVICES OF CONSULTANTS BY SSI UNITS

(a) General

The general reasons for not using consultants as reported by the SSI respondents who have not used the services in the past, has been analysed and the same are presented in Table 4.25.

TABLE 4.25

Reasons for not using consultants by the SSI units

Rank	*Reason*	*No. of units*	%
I	In house capability is available	10	48
II	Competent consultants are not available	08	38
III	Do not have any management problems	06	29
IV	Consultants are too costly	05	24
V	Consultants are not reliable	02	10
VI	They are not suitable to our needs	01	05

Thus, it may be seen that according to the users (SSI units) main reasons for not using consultants are non availability of competent consultants, high cost of service, lack of reliability and unsuitability for SSI units in that order of importance.

(b) Reasons for not utilising the services of the management consultants by the SSI units in the post production period even when they are not doing well

The respondent entrepreneurs were asked to indicate the reasons for not availing the services of the management consultants in the post production period inspite of the fact that most of them are not doing well. They were also requested to rank these reason in order of their importance. The data received has been analysed and the relative importance of these reasons has been presented on page 150.

Therefore, according to SSI respondents bad quality of service, high cost of service, lack of awareness amongst SSI entrepreneurs about the role and benefits of management consultancy services, inflexible approach of consultants regarding fee etc., inability of SSI entrepreneurs to identify their real management/technical problems and absence of any compulsion to hire consultants during post production period unlike pre-production period for taking financial and other benefits are major reasons for lower utilisation of management consultants by SSI units.

TABLE 4.26

Reasons for not availing the services of the management consultants during post-production period

Rank	*Reason*	*No of firms*	*%*
1	2	3	4
I	Right type of consultants are not available to the SSIs at reasonable cost.	45	88.23
II	Competent consultants with practical insight to solve the post production problems are not available.	27	52.94
III	Reliable and trustworthy consultants are difficult to get. They hardly have any professional ethics and leak information.	16	31.37
IV	They do not offer practical and feasible recommendations leading to non implementation.	11	21.57
V	Lesser qualified entrepreneurs do not realise the importance and benefits of management consultancy services and they are over confident about their abilities.	08	15.69
VI	Most of the SSIs units require techno-managerial and legal package but most of the consultants are basically project consultants and do not have any managerial skills. Even the chartered accountants only know about accounts and are hardly aware about project or management consultancy though they may call themselves management consultants.	04	07.84
VII	In India the consultants are not flexible in charging fee like their counterparts in developed countries who may even charge for one hour. Here they charge same fee as they may charge from large scale units with large resources.	03	05.88

cont...

1	2	3	4
VIII	SSI entrepreneurs do not understand their real management problems and their impact on the profitability of the unit.	03	05.88
IX	Engaging project consultants for arranging loans and other facilities is a compulsion for the SSI units but after production starts , there is no such compulsion.	02	03.92
X	Consultants do not approach the SSI units with their credentials hence they do not know about them.	02	03.92
XI	Consultants delay recommendations and are not available on demand.	02	03.92
XII	Less qualified entrepreneurs find it difficult to deal with highly qualified consultants due to difference in the background.	01	01.94
XIII	Some SSIs do not want to grow.	01	01.94
XIV	There is no consultancy culture in India.	01	01.94

However, reasons given by the SSI associations have been analysed and the position is presented below.

TABLE 4.27

Reasons for not utilising the services of the management consultants by the SSI units in the post production period (Rated by the Industry associations)

S.No.	*Reasons*	*No of associations*	*%*
1	The consultants are not having down to earth approach and are too theoretical keeping in view the status of SSI and some time give reports containing unrealistic estimates.	04	57.14
2	They are too costly and do not have flexible approach in charging fee on hourly basis as in developed countries.	04	57.14

cont...

1	2	3	4
3	Most of the entrepreneurs can not follow the sophisticated techniques suggested by the consultants and can not apply these recommendations.	01	14.29
4	The consultants suggest a lot of paper work for which no entrepreneur has time.	01	14.29
5	The consultants have inflated ego and do not consider them as part of the unit.	01	14.29
6	Illiterate entrepreneurs do not realise the importance of management consultant's services for their units	01	14.29
7	SSI units do not want to grow due to incentives of remaining a small units.	01	14.29

According to the industry associations too theoretical approach of the consultants coupled with the high cost of service deter the SSI units from approaching consultants. Consultants suggest difficult systems and a lot of paper work both of which are difficult for the SSI entrepreneurs to implement. Also the entrepreneurs having lower qualifications who are in majority in the rural areas are not able to appreciate the benefits of appointing a management consultant to solve the problems of their units. Thus SSI associations feel that bad quality of service and lack of awareness amongst SSI entrepreneurs about benefits of management consultancy services for SSI units, are two most important reasons for lower utilisation of these services by SSI units followed by lack of incentive to SSI units to grow.

Therefore, it can be concluded that according to user group bad quality of service, high cost of service, lack of awareness amongst SSI entrepreneurs about the role and benefits of management consultancy services, inflexible approach of consultants regarding fee etc., inability of SSI entrepreneurs to identify their real management/technical problems and absence of any compulsion to hire consultants during post production period unlike pre-production period for taking financial and other benefits are major reasons for lower utilisation of management consultants by SSI units.

4.28 SUGGESTIONS OF THE SSI ENTREPRENEURS TO IMPROVE THE UTILISATION OF MANAGEMENT CONSULTANCY SERVICES BY THE SSI UNITS

The respondent SSI entrepreneurs were asked to suggest ways and means to improve the utilisation of consultancy services by SSIs. The suggestions given by them have been analysed and presented below ranked in order of their importance.

TABLE 4.28

Suggestions of the SSI entrepreneurs to improve the utilisation of the management consultancy services by SSIs

S.N.	*Suggestion*	*No. of firms*
1	2	3
I	**Quality of consultancy service (Benefits vs cost) should be improved by taking following steps.**	**53**
(i)	Consultants have to first prove that their service will lead to better results and improvement in the performance of the clients unit.	15
(ii)	Consultants should be thoroughly trained and impaneled only after proper screening by the financial institutions, DICs , and their own associations and industry associations.	13
(iii)	Consultants have to show full trust, dependability and commitment to the growth of their client units.	07
(iv)	They should be thoroughly aware of the ground realities under which SSI units operate to enable them to give practical suggestions.	07
(v)	Consultants should come down to the level of their clients to understand their real problems and then give their suggestions and convince the clients about the practicability of the recommendations.	04

cont...

1	2	3
(vi)	Consultants should be able to provide technical. Managerial and legal services under one roof may be by forming a team.	04
(vii)	They should be able to suggest methods to reduce cost after a quick study.	01
(viii)	Perhaps a person who is less qualified but well experienced in the affairs of SSI units may be able to give better service than a well qualified but less experienced person.	01
(ix)	They should keep themselves up to date	01
II	**The cost of consultancy can be reduced by following steps**	**28**
(i)	Retainer consultancy to 4 or 5 SSI units can reduce the cost. Fee can be lump sum say Rs 2000 to Rs 10000 per month depending upon the payment capacity or 1% of sales or % of profit.	10
(ii)	Solo consultants with all-round ability (technical, managerial and legal) and nil overheads may be able to give cheaper service.	05
(iii)	Cost of project consultancy may be subsidised by the govt.	05
(iv)	Consultants should avoid paper work and should follow cheaper methods.	04
(v)	Less qualified (diploma holders) could be trained locally to work as consultants to SSIs under the guidance of an expert available at the regional level to reduce high cost	01
(vi)	Retired persons may be able to provide cheaper service	01
(vii)	TCOs could provide cheaper service.	01
(viii)	Cost can be reduced by serving a cluster of units at a place or giving them joint training.	01
III	**Consultants should market their services by resorting to following steps.**	**23**
(i)	Consultants should approach SSIs directly with their track records and references.	12
(iii)	SSIs should be made aware about the benefits of the consultancy services by the industry or the management consultants associations	05

cont...

1	2	3
(iii)	Consultants should approach industry associations for their empenelment.	01
(iv)	Prototype consultancy package could be prepared especially for the SSIs and marketed.	01
(v)	Regional data about the consultants along with details of services being given by them should be made available to the SSIs to make aware about them.	01
(vi)	Entrepreneurial development programmes should include a capsule on importance of management consultancy for SSIs.	01
(vii)	Management consultants for small business should establish their separate institute to solve their problems and market their services.	01
(viii)	Due publicity should be given to their services.	01
IV	**Other recommendations.**	**13**
(i)	In case of retainership following practices could be followed	07
	(a) Visit the client twice a week	02
	(b) Visit the client once a week	02
	(c) Regular service like chartered accountants	01
	(d) Should not have fee oriented approach	01
	(e) Should work as a insider and should work with full confidence.	01
(ii)	Consultancy needs of the SSIs be thoroughly understood	04
	(a) Problems are mostly integrated hence diagnostic study needed	02
	(b) Problems are strategic in nature and hence long term.	01
	(c) New units require project and old units management consultancy.	01
(iii)	Parent units should advice their ancillaries.	01
(iv)	SSIs should train their supervisors	01

Thus, according to respondent SSI units utilisation of management consultancy services by SSU units during post production period can be improved provided the quality of service is improved, cost of service is reduced and services are marketed properly with the help of steps suggested above.

Respondent SSI associations were also asked to suggest ways and means to improve the usage of consultancy services by the SSI units. As usual they had a tendency to go to the external factors like the role of govt. and its various agencies. Therefore their suggestions have been analysed and presented in two parts i.e. management problems and the external problems and presented in this section. With regard to external reasons they were of the opinion that in order to improve the performance of SSI units they should unitedly place their problems generated out of govt. policies before the govt. and should try to get such anti-SSI policies amended. Also labour laws should change and govt. should subsidise expenditure incurred by SSIs on land and electricity. Nayyar committee report on working capital financing should be implemented by the FIs. Govt. should continue the incentive to the SSI sector as it provides employment Development of agro-based SSI units may be encouraged for the benefit the farmers and rural people and reduce disparity in income. SSIs may go far networking for exploiting the core competencies and govt. purchases should go to the SSI units. These are typical prescriptions of the trade associations one hears. Since this study only concerns with the management problems of SSI which can be controlled without the help of Govt. no further comments have been made on these aspects. However it can be said that govt. can encourage development of professionalism and consultancy culture in the country by insisting on professional approach of govt. agencies and FIs which are also largely controlled by it. However suggestions of the industry associations to improve the usage of consultancy services by the small scale units involving internal initiatives are presented in Table 4.29.

It may be seen from the above that training of both the entrepreneur and the consultants is felt essential by the associations followed by other steps such as marketing through past references/work done registration with various agencies and going for retainer consultation. The external factors are not relevant to this study hence not commented upon . However the consultancy fee subsidy by the govt. may encourage the SSI units to go to consultants.

TABLE 4.29

Suggestions of SSI associations to improve the usage of consultancy services by small scale units

S.No.	*Suggestions for improving the use of consultancy services by the SSI units*
1	SSI units should adopt professional approach
2	Need based entrepreneurial training /business should be developed
3	The consultants should approach and develop the clients with the work done in the past
4	Consultants could go for registration with various agencies for better marketing and reliability.
5	They should create a package of service containing, technical, managerial and legal inputs
6	The consultants also require special education/training consisting of technical, managerial and legal inputs.
7	They should improve their reliability and be engaged on retainership basis.
8	The staff of the SSI units also required to be trained.
9	The consultants should be thoroughly trained in the SSI management so as to give practical recommendations.

Thus, the perception of SSI units presented above get enforced by the perception of their associations also and as such it can be concluded that according to user group utilisation of management consultancy services by SSU units during post production period can be improved provided the quality of service in improved, cost of service is reduced and services are marketed properly with the help of steps suggested above.

5

Perception of Financial Institutions

The seven financial institutions including commercial banks were interviewed by the researcher to have an independent and comparative views on important issues under investigation such as major management problems of SSI units, their major management consultancy needs, major reasons for lower utilisation of management consultancy services by the SSI units in the post production period, suggestions for improving the use of consultancy services by the SSI units. Their response has been analised and the position is as under:

5.1 MANAGEMENT PROBLEMS OF SSI UNITS

The financial institutions deal with the industrial units at all the stages. The SSI units approach them first for the term loan/working capital loan at the time of starting the unit and subsequently go to commercial banks for enhancing the cash credit limits when the sales picks up. Therefore the response of 7 financial institutions (5 commercial banks and 2 term lending institutions) about problems of SSIs has been taken and the position is presented below.

It may be seen that besides marketing, financial constraints and lack of integrity/diversion of funds have been perceived to be major problem of SSI units in that order of preference. The other important problem are entrepreneurial inadequacies, high cost of production, non viability due to capacity problems, financial mis-management and labour problems etc.

TABLE 5.1

Management problems of SSI units
(As rated by the financial institutions)

Rank	*Management problems*	*No. of FIs*	*%*
I	Competition is killing the SSI units	05	71.43
II	Insufficient funding by the FIs as per theoretical norms without taking into account ground realities forcing SSI to depend upon black money.	04	57.14
III	Poor integrity /diversion of funds	04	57.14
IV	Majority of the entrepreneurs do have capability to run the unit professionally	02	28.57
V	Bad quality /production problems	02	28.57
VI	Excessive repayment liability due to pre-production mistakes	01	12.29
VII	Non-availability of skilled manpower	01	12.29
VIII	High cost of production	01	12.29
IX	Low productivity due to labour problems	01	12.29
X	Non-viability due to capacity bottlenecks	01	12.29
XI	Financial mismanagement	01	12.29
XII	Undirected diversification	01	12.29

5.2 ACTUAL MANAGEMENT CONSULTANCY NEEDS OF SSI UNITS

The real management consultancy needs as perceived by the financial institutions are indicated below.

TABLE 5.2

Real management consultancy needs of SSI units

Rank	*Consultancy needs*	*No of FIs*	*%*
I	Marketing help for growth of sales including mature advice on business strategy and product mix	06	85.71

cont....

Rank	*Consultancy needs*	*No of FIs*	*%*
II	Resource optimisation through analysis, identification of wastes and reduction of cost	05	71.43
III	Working capital advice	01	14.29
IV	Recruitment of competent manpower	01	14.29
V	Training to supervisor	01	14.29
VI	Remove quality defects	01	14.29
VII	Study of systems	01	14.29
VIII	Technical up-gradation	01	14.29
IX	Published materials for SSI	01	14.29

It may be concluded that according to industry associations marketing and resource optimisation are the major areas in which the SSI units require helps followed by other areas as indicated above.

5.3 REASONS FOR LOW UTILISATION OF MANAGEMENT CONSULTANCY SERVICES BY SSI UNITS

The reasons quoted by the FIs have been analysed and the results have been placed below.

TABLE 5.3

Reasons for not utilising the management consultants by SSI units

Rank	*Reasons*	*No of FIs*	*%*
I	The management consultants are mostly impractical, are not aware of the ground realities and are not competent to deal with the problem of SSI units. Also they do not follow the banking norms.	06	85.71
II	SSI entrepreneurs do not trust the consultants and hence do not disclose full information.	04	57.14

cont....

Rank	*Reasons*	*No of FIs*	*%*
III	SSI units do not want to grow beyond SSI limits just to avail incentives of small scales and do not have any incentive to professionalise.	02	28.57
IV	The SSI entrepreneurs think that they know better than the consultants.	01	14.29
V	They are too costly.	01	14.29

It may be seen from the above that according to the FIs, bad quality of consultancy service, lack of mutual trust lack of incentive to professionalise and grow, ego problems of SSI entrepreneurs and high cost of service are the major reasons for not availing consultancy services.

5.4 SUGGESTIONS TO IMPROVE THE UTILISATION OF CONSULTANCY SERVICES BY SSI UNITS

The Financial Institutions have given following suggestions.

(1) New generation of professional entrepreneurs will go for management consultancy services so they should first approach such entrepreneurs and then get a good reference from them after satisfying them.

(2) SSI units should not treat MBAs as waste.

(3) The commercial banks have over 27000 branches all over India located in the rural and urban areas. Therefore the branch manager who deals with the small units also could motivate SSI units to go for management consultancy and there help could be taken.

(4) Banks should finance consultancy fee.

(5) Banks/term lending institutions could make a panel of consultants after due screening and circulate that list to all their branches. This could be done by the lead bank in a district.

(6) Branch managers of banks should be trained in the utility of management consultants as it may be beneficial to banks also as the improved performance of the SSI units will improve the recovery of loans.

(7) Banks do not have problems of deposits. They have problems in locating good units whom they can advance loan. Therefore the growth of SSI units with the help of management consultants will increase their potential to lend and reduce NPAs.

(8) The state director of industries should also make a panel of management consultants and the list could go to DICs. Also DICs could make such list at local basis.

(9) The industries associations should also maintain a panel of management consultants and encourage their members to utilise their services.

(10) The consultants should have very strong ethics not only for well being of their clients but also for the public funds.

(11) The consultants should be trained thoroughly in the SSI working.

(12) Retainer consultation is considered to be better than assignment basis because it makes the consultant partner in the progress of the unit.

(13) Govt. should not give any incentives to SSI units as people go only for the incentives and not for any other reasons. Rather such incentive for being small should be withdrawn so that the SSI units are forced to professionalise.

Thus it could be said that increasing the awareness of the SSI entrepreneurs about usefulness of management consultancy services for SSI units through training and marketing of these services, improving quality of services by developing professional ethics and training of the consultants, withdrawal of incentive for remaining small, financing consultancy fee considering it as an remuneraive investment in future and going for retainership are needed for improving the utilisation of management consultancy services by SSI units.

5.5 GENERAL COMMENTS OF FINANCIAL INSTITUTIONS

The financial institutions have given following general comments:

(1) Now the working of domestic banks have become very difficult due to tough competition from foreign banks and priority sector lending.

(2) Frequent changes in the govt. policies creates mistrust.

(3) 90% of the SSI units utilise the services of CAs for taking loans etc.

(4) It is not possible for the banks to include any conditions of compulsory engagement of management consultants in case of defaults etc. due to tough competition from other banks. This is only possible when RBI enforces uniform policy in this regard. Banks have funds which they have to lend to somebody.

(5) Only complicated credit proposals are send to the consultancy cell of the bank located in the HQ or regional offices.

(6) Now the banks are insisting on the security to coup up with the uncertainty of business as many of the branch officers have got charge sheets for defaults of the party.

(7) This study should identify real consultancy needs of the SSI units.

(8) Consultants should be in private sector.

(9) The consultants can help only when they have proper caliber.

(10) Black money creates more complications for the banks.

(11) The annual statements are window dressed with low profits and low asset base. So it becomes difficult for the bank to grant higher credit.

6

Comparative Analysis of Perceptions/ Practices of Users, Suppliers and Third Groups

The perceptions of the three groups of respondents, i.e. suppliers, users and financial institutions and various practices reported by them with regard to consultancy services have been compared in reference to the issues mentioned below and the inferences have been drawn by the researcher.

1. Relative importance of various management problems of SSI units.
2. Relative importance of the real management consultancy needs of the SSI units.
3. The management problems of the SSI units vis-à-vis their real consultancy needs.
4. The actual demand of management consultancy services by SSI units (actual consultancy needs) vis-à-vis supply of such serves (the consultancy services being made available by the management consultants).
5. Actual management consultancy needs of SSIs vis-à-vis the consultancy services actually availed by them.
6. The reasons for not utilising the management consultancy services by the SSI units and their relative importance .

7. The relative importance of major reasons for lower utilisation of consultancy services by the SSI units vis-à-vis major reasons for not serving the SSI sector as reported by consultants.
8. The relative importance of the major problems of consultants while dealing with SSI units vis-à-vis major problems of SSI units while dealing with consultants.
9. Methods of charging consultancy fee by consultants vis-à-vis methods employed by user SSI units to pay the consultancy fee in the past.
10. Mode of engagement reported by consultants vis-à-vis mode of engagement desired by SSI units.
11. Extent of use of consultants by SSI units vis-à-vis extent of service to SSI units by consultants.
12. Sector of Consultants available vis-à-vis sector of consultants used by SSI respondents.
13. The usefulness of management consultants in improving the performance of SSI units.
14. The suggestions to improve the utilisation of management consultancy services by SSI units and their relative importance.
15. Relative importance of the suggestions given to improve the quality of consultancy services to SSI sector.
16. Relative importance of various suggestions for a viable marketing strategy.
17. Relative importance of suggestions to reduce the cost of consultancy services to the SSI sector.

6.1 RELATIVE IMPORTANCE OF VARIOUS MANAGEMENT PROBLEMS OF SSI UNITS

The rating given by suppliers, users and third group i.e. the financial institutions has been analysed and discussed in the respective section. It may be seen that according to user group marketing is the major problem area followed by finance and personnel. However the supplier group feels that mistakes done during pre-production period are prime cause of all the problems, followed by financial problems like lack of proper utilisation of the resources and lack of costing system and marketing. The financial institutions also rate marketing as the major problem followed by finance and lack of integrity/ diversion of funds/entrepreneurial inadequacy. Thus there is gap in the perceptions of the user and supplier groups.

The pre-production mistakes have been rated as first only by the supplier group. But is worth mentioning that the user group was asked to indicate and rate the post production management problems. Therefore pre-production mistakes can be accepted as undisputed problems common to all the groups and only post production management problems could be ascertained and rated.

Thus taking into account the perceptions of all groups, it may be concluded that marketing, finance and then personnel are the most important management problems before the SSI units which they may like to solve may be with outside help.

6.2 RELATIVE IMPORTANCE OF THE REAL MANAGEMENT CONSULTANCY NEEDS OF SSI UNITS

As per the perception of the user group, marketing, finance and personnel management are the major consultancy needs that order. However individual consultancy needs in order of importance are suggesting market development plan including sales promotion, assists in getting loans, optimal use of cost reduction and training of entrepreneurs and his staff. However the supplier group rates projects services first followed by market development, financial services including cost reduction and training to SSI entrepreneurs &. their staff. The financial institution also rate the marketing as the most importance service followed by finance, recruitment of competent manpower and training of staff etc.

The project services are rated first only by the supplier group, the reason being that in case of user and third group, only post production services have been got rated. Therefore the project services will always remain important at the conception stage to the implementation stage and any serious mistake committed at this stage may make the unit non viable for ever.

On the basis of above analysis, it can be concluded that at the initial stage the project management services remain critical but after the production has commenced the marketing services will become the most important service required by the SSI units followed by financial services including cost reduction and working capital management, optimal use of resources and the personnel services including training to the entrepreneurs and their staff.

6.3 MANAGEMENT PROBLEMS OF SSI UNITS VIS -A-VIS THEIR REAL CONSULTANCY NEEDS

It is seen that the marketing, finance and the personnel management services are the major internal management problem areas, whereas the real management needs are project services at the initial stage then marketing, finance and then personnel services. Thus there is no perceptible difference between management problems and the management consultancy needs. The project management problems do not appear in management problems because of the fact that the respondents were asked to rate only the internal management problems of post production stage. Secondly there can be no dispute about the need of good project services at the project conception to commissioning stage.

6.4 THE ACTUAL MANAGEMENT CONSULTANCY NEEDS VIS -A -VIS THE CONSULTANCY SERVICES BEING MADE AVAILABLE BY MANAGEMENT CONSULTANTS

The required management consultancy needs are rated as project services in the pre-production stage and marketing, finance and personnel services (mostly training) during post production stage. Whereas the services actually available in order of importance are project management services, general management, personnel management, production, marketing, finance and then others. Thus except the project management all other services needed are not being extended by the consultants.

Whereas the marketing management services are rated to most important consultancy need of the SSI units, they rank fourth in the post production consultancy services being extended by the consultants. Similarly the need for the financial services including cost reduction and working capital management are ranked second but on the availability side it is rated fifth. The general management services ranks third on the need side but second on the supply side.

The demand for the training services is ranked fourth but its supply is ranked second. The demand for production management services are raked very low by all the respondent groups but its supply is ranked above marketing and the finance.

Thus it is seen that the supply of consultancy services is not as per the demand and there is wide gap for various types of services. The consultants have to bridge this gap if they wish to grow.

6.5 ACTUAL MANAGEMENT CONSULTANCY NEEDS VIS-À-VIS THE CONSULTANCY SERVICES ACTUALLY AVAILED BY USER SSI UNITS.

The actual consultancy needs are project services followed by marketing, finance including optimal use of resources and personnel services whereas the services availed are project services, marketing, personnel and then finance. Here the share of project services is very large (75%) and the share of other post production management consultancy services is extremely low. This is probably due to non availability of desired services as indicated in the preceding para.

6.6 THE REASONS FOR LOW UTILISATION OF MANAGEMENT CONSULTANCY SERVICES BY SSI UNITS AND THEIR RELATIVE IMPORTANCE

Besides the reasons such as availability of in house capability and absence of management problems, the reasons for not using management consultants have been rated by the user group in order of importance as non availability of competent consultants, high cost of service, lack of awareness of the SSI entrepreneurs about the benefits of management consultancy services for SSI units, inflexible approach of the consultants with regard to fee etc., inability of SSI entrepreneurs in identifying their management/technical problems and no compulsions during the post production period, unreliability of the consultants and unsuitability of the consultants to their needs. However supplier group feels that non awareness of the SSI units about the utility of the management consultancy services is the main reason for low use followed by high cost of service, lack of expertise in consultants needed for SSI units and the mistrust of the entrepreneurs on the consultants. The financial institutions also feel that impractical approach of the consultants, lack of trust of SSI entrepreneurs on the consultants, lack of incentive to grow, the ego problem of the entrepreneurs and high cost of service are the main reasons for low use. Thus there is perception gap in various groups.

However keeping in view the importance of perception of the customers it may be concluded that inadequate quality of service, high cost, mistrust between the SSI units and the consultants, lack of awareness in the SSI units about the benefits of consultancy service in improving the performance of the SSI units and lack of interest of the entrepreneurs in growth of their units, are the main reasons of low utilisation of the consultancy services by the SSI units in the post-production period.

6.7 THE MAJOR REASONS FOR LOWER UTILISATION OF CONSULTANCY SERVICES BY SSI UNITS VIS-À-VIS MAJOR REASONS FOR NOT SERVING SSI SECTOR BY CONSULTANTS

The supplier group reports that lack of appreciation of the usefulness of the management consultancy service on the part of SSI entrepreneurs in solving their management problems, high cost of service and the difficulty in solving the problems inherited by the SSI units due to mistakes committed during the project conception and implementation stage are the major reasons for not serving the SSI sector. Whereas the reasons for not availing the services of the management consultants as reported by user group and the third group are bad quality and high cost of service, mistrust, lack of awareness about the benefits of consultancy services amongst the SSI units and the lack of interest in the entrepreneurs in the growth of the units.

Therefore the perception gap between the users and suppliers of management consultancy services is clearly seen from the above. The main concern of the consultants is lack of awareness amongst SSI entrepreneurs about the benefits of management consultancy services and the problem of payment due to high cost whereas the concern of the users are quality as well as cost. However it will be prudent to believe the customer and advice the consultant to improve themselves.

6.8 THE MAJOR PROBLEMS OF CONSULTANTS WHILE DEALING WITH SSI UNITS VIS-À-VIS MAJOR PROBLEMS OF SSI UNITS WHILE DEALING WITH CONSULTANTS

The major problems of the consultants with SSI units as reported by them in order of importance are lack of awareness about the benefits of the consultancy services and resultant view that expenditure of consultancy is total waste, payment problems, unprofessional approach of the SSI entrepreneurs, non- realisation of the viability problems of the consultants, high degree of mistrust and resultant non-disclosure of vital information required for giving practical suggestions, hesitation in implementing the recommendations, tough competition with scrupulous elements, going to consultant at the last resort when the problems become difficult to solve, ignorance of the entrepreneurs about their problems and lack of expertise in running the unit. However as per the user SSI units who had used the services of consultants in the past, the major problems are bad quality of service which included delay in implementation, paper oriented, bureaucratic approach on the part of Govt. consultants and impractical/theoretical suggestions. So there is wide gap in the perception of users and suppliers of consultancy service. Here the quality and the cost of service are two main elements which should be acknowledge by consultants. However consultants also may not be entirely wrong and SSI entrepreneurs have to also improve their awareness about the benefit of management consultancy services. However consultant have to first prove their wroth to gain the confidence of the customers and have to convince them about the benefit of consultancy through demonstration of real benefits of the consultancy services extended by them in the past. We can not blame the customer for his ignorance.

6.9 METHOD OF CHARGING CONSULTANCY FEE BY CONSULTANTS VIS-À-VIS METHOD EMPLOYED BY USER SSI UNITS TO PAY THE CONSULTANCY FEE IN THE PAST

The consultants have ranked the methods of changing consultancy fee in order of importance as consultants man days, percentage of project cost, lump sum, percentage of sales, percentage of savings etc. Whereas dominant method employed by SSI units for paying consultancy fee were lump sum basis, consultants man days basis, retainership, percentage of project cost and percentage of loan amount. So in actual practice the SSI units have preferred to pay on lump sum basis. The consultants may take note of this fact.

6.10 MODE OF ENGAGEMENT REPORTED BY CONSULTANTS VIS-À-VIS MODE OF ENGAGEMENT DESIRED BY SSI UNITS

The modes of engagement reported by the consultants in order of importance are assignment basis (57%), retainership basis (10%) and on mix methods (33%), whereas the majority of the customers-SSI units (52.90%) are in favour of retainer consultancy followed by the assignment basis (35.30%) and mixed method i.e. assignment basis for the new units and retainership basis during post production period.

Thus customers want long term association of the consultants against the present practice of engagement on assignment basis. Thus it may be said that clients wish to have continued relationship to have dependable and better understanding of the clients needs etc.

6.11 EXTENT OF USE OF CONSULTANTS BY SSI UNITS VIS-À-VIS EXTENT OF SERVICE TO SSI UNITS BY CONSULTANTS

It is seen that 65.35% of the consultants serve the SSI sector and 59.09% of them have less than 50% of their annual consultancy turn over from the SSI units. On the client side also 58.82% of the respondent SSI units used the services of consultants. Therefore there is no perceptive gap in this area.

6.12 SECTOR OF CONSULTANTS AVAILABLE VIS-À-VIS SECTOR OF THE CONSULTANTS USED BY SSI RESPONDENTS

It is a fact that majority of the consultants are in the private sector followed by the public, govt. and autonomous sectors. On the utilisation side also 25 out of 30 SSI units took help from Pvt. sector (80%), 2 from public sector and 2 from govt. sector. Thus private sector plays significant role in this area.

6.13 THE AWARENESS ABOUT USEFULNESS OF MANAGEMENT CONSULTANTS IN IMPROVING THE PERFORMANCE OF SSI UNITS

Whereas majority of the consultants as well as IMCI feel that most of the SSI units are not aware of usefulness of the management consultants in improving the performance of SSI units and suggest the same, most of the SSI units (90%) do believe that professional management practices as well as management consultants could improve the performance of SSI units provided that consultants improve quality of their service, bring down the cost of their service and make them suitable to the special consultancy needs of the SSI sector. Thus, there is wide gap in the perceptions of the users and the suppliers of the consultancy services. However it is worth mentioning that the sample is biased in favour of urban based SSIs units owned by professionally qualified and well experienced entrepreneurs. Therefore their level of awareness is bound to be much higher then majority of the SSI entrepreneurs located in ruler/semi-urban areas having moderate academic background of importance are taking a number of steps to improve the awareness of the entrepreneurs about the utility of management consultancy services and to remove their mental block, marketing the services, reduce the cost of service, increasing promoters commitment for the growth of the SSIs, improving the quality of service and strengthening the public/Govt. sector consultants.

The major suggestions of the user group in order of importance are, improving the quality of service, reducing the cost of service and marketing the service besides going for retainership and effective diagnosis of the problems of the SSI clients. According to the FIs cost reduction, increasing awareness of the SSIs about the benefits of management consultancy services, marketing of the services with the help of commercial bank/FIs etc., improving quality of service by development of very strong professional ethics about the welfare of their clients and the public funds and training the consultants and entrepreneurs, withdrawal of the incentive for remaining small to force them to professionalise and use the services of the consultants, financing the expenditure on consultancy fee considering it to be an investment in future and resorting to mode of retainer consultancy can improve the utilisation of management consultancy services by SSI units.

Thus it could be concluded that to improve the use of management consultancy services by the SSI sector during the post production period, the consultants have to improve the quality of their services, increase the awareness of the SSI entrepreneurs about the benefits of consultancy services through marketing efforts, reduce the cost of service, develop strong professional ethics and resort to retainer consultancy. Also the commitment of the entrepreneurs is to be increased by proper training about identification of their real problems, selection and use of consultants. It may be seen that there is significant gap in the perception of the users and supplier of management consultancy services as well as other parties.

6.14 RELATIVE IMPORTANCE OF THE SUGGESTIONS GIVEN TO IMPROVE THE QUALITY OF SERVICE

According to the supplier group the quality of service could be improved by thorough training of the consultants by IMCI and by gaining practical experience about the working of the SSI sector. However, according to the user group the quality of their services can be improved through in depth training of the consultants, their enlistment by concerned parties only after proper screening, development of reliability and commitment in growth of their clients, development of full awareness about the ground realities of SSI working, offering simple and practical suggestions, marketing need based packages to this sector and updating their knowledge. FIs emphasise need for strong professional ethics and again emphasis training of the consultants.

Thus, it can be concluded that in depth training of consultants in the practical aspects of the SSI working, impaneled after thorough screening, gaining experience of SSI working, developing the trustworthiness, dependability and commitment for development of their clients, providing simple and practical suggestions and flexible service packages with flexible cost of consultancy can improve the quality of service.

6.15 RELATIVE IMPORTANCE OF VARIOUS SUGGESTIONS FOR A VIABLE MARKETING STRATEGY

The marketing of consultancy services involve steps such as increasing the awareness of the customer about the utility of the services and making them aware about the existence of the suppliers. For increasing the awareness the supplier group has suggested brain storming sessions with the SSI entrepreneurs preferably at various industrial estates, seminars / panel discussions by the IMCI, frequent interactions between the consultants and the clients and training to the entrepreneurs about the benefits of consultancy services. The user group suggest that consultant should resort to direct selling with their track records and they could be made aware about the benefits of the consultancy services by the IMCI and the industry associations and should be impaneled by industry associations and other related institutions. They wish to have data about the consultants along with the services being given by them. They also suggest that the entrepreneurial development programs may include a capsule on the availability and use of management consultancy services and a separate institute for consultants serving SSIs. IMCI also suggests joint meeting of the industry associations and their members with the consultants and circulation of list of consultants who wish to serve the SSI units to all concerned. The industry associations also feel that professional approach of entrepreneurs training about the benefits of consultancy, approaching clients with past work done, registration with concern agencies may be part of marketing strategy. FIs want consultants to take help of vast network of commercial banks who normally deal with the SSI units even during post production period and suggest that the branch managers may be trained in this area. They are also in favour of enlistment of consultants with the concern agencies and going for retainership.

It may be seen from the above that the consultants and the IMCI prefer joint meetings of the local chapters of IMCI and the industry associations for creating awareness, therefore it becomes the most important suggestion. Training to the entrepreneurs in importance of management consultancy services and use of consultants has been stressed by the consultants, SSI units and their associations. Consultants suggest frequent interactions but not the others. Empenelment of consultants by the agencies responsible for industrial development and financing has been stressed by SSIs, their associations and FIs. Direct marketing has been also suggested by SSIs and their association.

Thus, it can be concluded that awareness of the entrepreneurs about the importance of management consultancy services could be enhanced by joint meeting, seminars/panel discussions with the entrepreneurs and their associations, enlistment of consultants after thorough screening and circulation of list to all associations and other bodies like FIs, DICs etc., training to the entrepreneurs about the usefulness of the management consultancy and how to diagnose their problems, frequent interaction with the entrepreneurs and use of network of commercial banks in approaching the SSI units.

The other steps as suggested by the consultants are working for SSI units having professional entrepreneurs and then getting references from them and then going to other units with past track records as suggested by the SSI units developing long term retainer relationships to get more such references. The SSI units also confirm that reference with good track records is essential for the acceptability of the consultants and further suggest development of need based packages for the SSI units. They feel that IMCI is hardly interested in the development of management consultancy profession to suit the needs of SSI sector, therefore a separate association for consultants desirous of serving SSI sector may be established. The industry associations also put emphasis on consultants approaching the clients with past track records and also developing special package for this sector .

Thus, it can be seen that other steps may include using past references, developing special packages and marketing them, going for retainer consultancy for long term relations. The consultants could establish a separate association for them if IMCI is not able to meet their requirements.

6.16 RELATIVE IMPORTANCE OF VARIOUS SUGGESTIONS TO REDUCE THE COST OF CONSULTANCY SERVICES TO THE SSI SECTOR

The consultants suggest Govt., subsidy/financing of cost of consultancy, retainer consultancy to 4 or 5 SSI units on part time basis, sharing of fee by the industry associations and the DICs, solo consultation, consultation by retired persons to reduce the cost of service. These steps are supported by the SSI units also who also feel that less qualified person with good experience of SSI working may be useful. These could work under the supervision of an expert. The service of SSI units in a cluster may also reduce the cost. FIs support the idea of retainer consultancy.

In view of the above it could be concluded that retainer consultation with 4 or 5 SSI units at a time, solo practice without any overheads, use of retired persons as consultant, use of prototype services, subsidy by the Govt. paper less and cheap consultation methods by the consultants, use of lesser qualified person as consultants under the supervision of an expert can reduce the cost of service considerably and then SSI units may go for use of consultants.

7

Conclusions and Recommendations

The research study has led to following conclusions, inferences and recommendations. These are based on the results of literature research as well as field research conducted by the researcher.

7.1 CONCLUSIONS

On the basis of the findings of the literature survey reported in the second chapter and the field survey conducted by the researcher as per predetermined research methodology and results of analysis presented from third to sixth chapters, following conclusions can be drawn about the related attributes/features of management consultancy services in general and for small scale sector in particular and small scale industrial units taking into account the perceptions of the supplier, user and third group, i.e. financial institutions about quality and allied dimensions of management consultancy services for SSI units in India. This has formed the base for drawing inferences for facilitating recommendation forwarded subsequently.

7.1.1 Management Consultancy Services

1. The management consultants are mostly concentrated in the metropolitan cities followed by state capitals and important industrial towns, whereas majority of the SSI units are located in

smaller towns and rural areas. Therefore, there is geographical gap in demand and the supply of consultancy services.

2. Majority of the consultants (95%) are operating in the private sector followed by the autonomous sector (productivity councils), public sectors (TCOs) and Govt. sector (SISIs).
3. Most of the consultancy organisations are either sole proprietorships or partnerships (97.50%) remaining forms of organisations being only 2.5%.
4. About 90% of the consultancy firms have annual turn over of less than Rs. 5 lacs. The total number of the consultants employed by 103 respondents consultancy organisations comes to 960, therefore the average employment per firm comes to less than 10. Since the sample is biased towards larger public sector(TCOs)/Govt. sector consultancy organisations, this figure may not be reliable and it could be somewhere between 2 to 3 consultants per consultancy firm.
5. About 85% of the principal consultants are professionally qualified.
6. 94% of the principal consultants have experience of over 15 years.
7. In 85% cases consultancy firms employ less than 10 consultants excluding the part time consultants out of which 30% are solo practitioners. Therefore, there is no likelihood of any organisational complexity.
8. Majority of the consultancy firms (over 63%) employ part time consultants.
9. The professionals like engineering and management graduates, chartered/cost accountants dominate as consultants (63.90%).
10. Majority of the consultancy firms (70%) employ consultants having experience over 15 years.

However 45.90% of the consultants have experience of over 15 years.

11. The consultancy profession is at present dominated by the technocrats (42.10%) due to pre- dominance of project consultancy. Only 32% are management graduates.
12. Project consultancy is the main area of consultation during the pre production period. However during the post production period general management, personnel, production, marketing and finance are the major areas of consultation.
13. Majority of the consultants charge consultancy fee on the basis of consultants man days followed by other methods such as percentage of project cost, lump sum percentage of loan and sometimes sales.
14. Majority of the consultants (90%) get engaged on assignment basis followed by the retainer basis(43%).
15. 65% of the consultants had served the SSI units in the past and majority of them (60%) have less than 50% of their turn over from the SSI sector and as such they depend upon medium/large scale industrial units for survival. However the sample being biased in favour of consultants who serve SSI units, it can be concluded that majority of the consultants do not serve SSI units.
16. As per the consultants they do not serve SSI units due to payment problems, lack of awareness amongst SSI entrepreneurs about the utility of management consultancy services in improving the performance of SSI units and ignorance of the SSI entrepreneurs about their real problems.
17. The major problems of the consultants during consultation with SSI units in order of importance are lack of awareness of the entrepreneurs about the benefits of management consultancy services/

considering the expenditure on consultancy a total waste, payment problems, unprofessional approach of the entrepreneurs, non realisation of the viability problems of the consultants, high degree of mistrust and resultant non disclosure of information considered vital for giving useful advice, hesitation in implementing the recommendations, tough competition from unscrupulous consultants, going to the consultant at the last stage when the problem becomes almost incurable like going to a doctor when the patient is dying, ignorance about their real problems and lack of expertise on the part of the entrepreneurs in running the unit professionally.

18. According to the consultants the use of management consultancy services by the SSI units during the post production period can be increased if the awareness of the entrepreneurs about the benefits of the management consultancy services can be increased by suitable methods and their mental block about the consultants is removed, the services are marketed properly, cost of service is reduced, the commitment of the entrepreneurs about the growth of their units is increased and the quality of service is improved.

7.1.2 Small Scale Industrial Units in India

1. It is seen that 82% of the SSI units did not employ the management graduate or diploma holders even when the sample is biased toward urban and organised SSI units. Therefore, barring the management capability of the entrepreneurs themselves, there is hardly any in-house management expertise available with the SSI units. The industry associations have further informed that majority of the SSI entrepreneurs are simple graduates and hardly 10% of the entrepreneurs are professionals. Therefore it can be concluded

that required in-house managerial expertise is mostly missing from the SSI sector. Therefore they should prema facie utilise the services of management consultants provided the quality and cost of such services suits them.

2. 72.55% of the respondent SSI units were not satisfied with their present level of performance. Thus, the findings of the earlier studies get confirmed.
3. Majority of the entrepreneurs (88.22%) believe that good management practice can solve their management problems. Though the sample is dominated by the professional entrepreneurs, the result may not be much different though the percentage may drop. Secondly with the likely increase in the number of professional entrepreneurs in future this perception will get strengthened.
4. According to the SSI entrepreneurs, marketing and finance are critical managerial problem areas followed by personnel, production and project management.
5. The consultancy needs of SSI sector as reported by the SSI units are also in the areas of marketing and finance followed by personnel, production and general management in that order of importance. The individual needs in order of importance are suggesting the market development (including sales) plan, assistance in getting short term/long term loans, suggest ways to optimise the use of funds, suggest cost reduction strategy training the entrepreneurs and their supervisors, analyse the market, rationalise the working capital management and identification of new market segments.
6. Only 60% of the SSI units used the services of consultants in the past.

7. According to them they are not utilising the services of management consultants due to non-availability of competent consultants at reasonable cost, lack of reliability and trust and unsuitability of the existing consultants to their special requirements.
8. Mostly services of Pvt. consultants (80%) are being used by SSI units followed by TCOs and SISIs.
9. Most of units (80%) used consultants for project consultancy just to get loan and 20% (12% of the total number of respondents) used consultants in the post production period. The project consultancy involved preparation of techno-economic feasibility reports, filling loan application, product development and project profile etc. The services availed at the post-production stage included marketing, networking, sales policy formulation export documentation, under marketing training under personnel management and formulation of a new company and computerisation under general management service.
10. Majority of the units (60%) paid fee on lump sum basis. The per consultants man days charge varies from even less than Rs.250 to over Rs. 5000/- depending upon the quality of consultants and the payment capacity of the user units. Retainer consultancy was not found to be so popular as yet.
11. Majority of the consultants (over 60%) took less than one month to complete the job.
12. In 30% cases the recommendations were not implemented due to lack of practicability of the suggestions given by the consultants.
13. Majority of the units (53%) were not satisfied with the services given to them by consultants, 63% of the units having satisfaction level of 50% or below.

Therefore the satisfaction level is quite low and hence the quality.

14. In most of the cases involving project consultancy, no identification of problem was involved as it was very clear the unit was to be established or company was to be formed. However in rest of the cases the symptoms such as shortage of cash, slowing down of exports, taxation problems with the Government forced them to go the consultants. Therefore proper diagnostic study was not done by any of the respondent entrepreneurs to know his real problems.
15. In majority of the cases (59.70%) the selection was due to previous relationship and in 21.45% cases due to intervention or at the suggestion of third party like financial institution/Govt. agency, only in 17.85% cases, the entrepreneur selected the consultant afresh. Thus the past/other references are the dominating factors in selection of consultants.
16. In majority of the cases (82%) the expectation was very clear i.e. getting loans or solving some legal/taxation problem. Only in 18% cases the entrepreneurs wanted to improve the efficiency, quality and sales. Thus intention to professionalise is hardly visible in SSI sector.
17. In 43% of the cases the expectations were not clearly stated by the entrepreneurs, the cases being basically post production consultancy assignments. Therefore the consultants had to workout the job on their own. This may be a cause of poor quality service.
18. In 73% cases consultancy contracts did not exist at all leading to confusion with regards to scope of work and the terms and conditions were not clear which might have led to misunderstanding.
19. The major short comings in the services as reported

by the SSI respondents were supply of all data related to technical and marketing aspects to the consultants by the SSI units, theoretical project estimates, failure of the consultants in convincing the bankers about the amount of loan required, bureaucratic approach of the Govt./public sector consultants, lack of practical inputs in the training programmes arranged by them and delay in completing the assignment.

20. The desired benefits came mostly in case of project consultancy as the unit got the loan and the unit was established. However the consultation involving the improvement in the existing level of performance in the post production period failed to produce the benefits to the desired extent in 40% of the cases.

21. The problems faced by the respondents entrepreneurs during the consultation process as reported by them were bureaucratic approach of govt. consultants, impractical suggestions leading to sickness and delays in completion of the assignment.

22. Majority of the units (60%) did not want to repeat the same consultant as they were not satisfied with the quality of service.

23. 90% of the respondent SSI units believed that management consultancy service can improve their performance provided the consultants improve the quality of their services.

24. 83% of the units preferred lump sum payment, 13% as percentage of sales and 3% as percentage of project cost. Most of them were ready to pay Rs 2000 per month as retainer charges to a consultant who may serve a number of SSI units side by side on part time and continuous basis and this figure may go to Rs 10000 per month for good consultants

depending upon the payment capacity of the unit.

25. Almost all the SSI respondents were of the view that the benefits from the consultants should be double than the cost of consultancy.
26. Majority of the units (52.90%) prefer retainership over assignment basis which may be only for project consultancy.
27. According to SSI entrepreneurs major reasons for not using the management consultants during the post production, in order of importance are non availability of competent consultants at the reasonable/affordable rates, unreliability of the consultant, their unsuitability to the needs of the SSI sector, failure of SSI entrepreneurs in understanding their real problems and likely benefits of the management consultancy services and inflexibility of the consultant in respect of consultancy fee etc.
28. The major suggestions of the SSI units to improve the use of management consultants, in order of importance are improving the quality of service, reducing the cost of service and marketing the services by the consultants.

7.1.3 The perception of allied groups and third group i.e. Financial Institutions

The responses allied groups i.e. IMCI and SSI Associations and the third group i.e. financial institutions about the important issues of this investigation i.e. major management problems of the SSI units during the post production period, their real consultancy needs, reasons for lower utilisation of services of management consultants during the post production period, their suggestions for improving the use of the services by the SSI units and their general comments .can be concluded as under.

7.1.3.1 The institute of management consultants of India

1. The major mistakes committed during the pre-production/project stage, sub-optimal use of available resources, marketing., entrepreneurial inadequacies, lack of costing systems and procedures, lack of training of entrepreneurs and supervisors, bad quality products, high inventories and financial constraints are the major problems of the SSI units.
2. The assistance in selecting a viable and realistic project and its implementation including the loan arrangements etc. during the pre-production period and market development study, recommending realistic strategies for optimal use of resources, cost reduction, provide need based training to the entrepreneurs and his staff, suggesting methods for improving the quality of products and better working capital management methods during the post production period are the major management consultancy needs of the SSI sector.
3. The SSI units, according to IMCI do not use consultants due to non awareness about the benefits of management consultancy services for them and high degree of mistrust of the SSI units on the management consultants.
4. IMCI suggests that management consultancy should be made compulsory by the Govt. for SSI units having availed loan beyond a limit as is case with the financial/cost audit and awareness about the likely benefits of management consultancy should be increased by various marketing efforts and list of consultants who wish serve SSI units, should be circulated to all concerned.
5. It is further seen that the IMCI does not has a proper system of screening the consultants before

it enlists them as its member and the member can claim to be certified management consultants. The institute has hardly about 300 members which is not even 2% of the total strength of the consultants available in India. The majority of its members are serving only large units on the plea of viability and payment problems from the SSI units.

7.1.3.2 Industry associations

In order to have the representative view of the SSI units (customer group) in face of an urban oriented relatively smaller size sample which suffers from many limitations, the researcher interviewed 07 SSI associations and their views on various issues can be summerised as under:

1. Marketing, resource utilisation are the two most critical problem area of the SSI sector followed by working capital management, labour problems entrepreneurial inadequacies and bad quality products during the post production period and mistakes committed during pre-production period..
2. Remedy pre-production mistakes, market development, suggestions for proper use of resources and cost reduction, suggesting simple control systems and training the entrepreneurs and their staff are the major consultancy needs of the SSI sector during post production period and loans etc. during the pre-production/expansion/ modernisation stage.
3. The SSI units do not use consultants during the post-production period due to highly theoretical/ impractical approach of the consultants, high cost of service and lack of awareness in the SSI entrepreneurs about the likely benefits of management consultancy services and consequently thinking the expenditure on consultancy a total waste. Also the small units are

hardly in a position to implement the complex systems suggested by the consultants who largely have experience of serving large and complex units.

4. The use of management consultancy services can be improved provided the entrepreneurs and the consultants are trained thoroughly in utilising and extending the services, services are marketed properly by the consultants with the help of enlistment with the concerned bodies (Industry associations, state directorate of industries, DICs, FIs and industrial development authorities), direct selling through past references and good track records, the cost of service is reduced and retainer consultancy is resorted to.
5. It was gathered from the associations that majority of the SSI units even located in the industrial estates employ less that 20 persons and have investment below Rs 10 lakhs. It is also reported that 90% of the entrepreneurs were non professionals. Therefore these units are hardly able to grasp the fast changes taking place in the market.

7.1.3.3 Financial institutions

1. According to them, marketing, financial constraints, poor integrity/diversion of funds, high cost of production, entrepreneurial inadequacies, bad quality of products, pre-operation mistakes like non- viability due to capacity problems and financing nonremunerative assets are the major problems of the SSI units in that order of importance.
2. Marketing, finance including optimal use of resources and cost reduction, training of the entrepreneurs and their staff, system studies and modernisation are the major consultancy needs.
3. SSI units do not use consultants due to bad quality of service, lack of mutual trust, high cost of service,

lack of incentives to SSI units to grow and unprofessional approach of the entrepreneurs .

4. In order to improve the use of management consultants by the SSI units during the post production period, the cost of service is to be reduced and marketing has to be stepped up with the help of the branch managers of the commercial banks may be after giving them proper training and enlisting consultants with them. The consultants should also enlist themselves with the industry associations, DICs, state directorate of industries, FIs etc. The consultants have to develop strong professional ethics about the development of their clients and also about the public money invested in the private sector. They are also to be trained to improve the quality of service and should go for retainer consultancy.
5. Now the domestic financial institutions are facing acute problems due to entry of foreign banks who have better freedom to opt for big accounts and as such most of the good customers are gravitating towards them due to bureaucratic approach of the Indian public sector banks who also have additional burden of priority sector lending. As such it is not possible for them to include any clause in the loan agreement about hiring of management consultant in case of failure of the unit to return the loan as per terms and conditions of the contract. It is only possible when RBI enforce it on all the banks/FIs uniformly. Secondly the consultancy cells of the commercial banks mostly serve as internal consultancy cells and deal with complicated loan cases and in rare cases render advice to SSI units. They have desired that this study should identify the real consultancy needs of the small scale sector.

7.1.4 Perceptions of user and supplier groups

The perceptions of the user and supplier groups about important aspects such as major management problems of the SSI units during the post production period, their real consultancy needs, reasons for not availing the services of management consultants during the post production period and their suggestions for improving the use of the services by the SSI units can be concluded as under.

7.1.4.1 The supplier group

(a) Management Problems of SSIs

Project conception and implementation stage mistakes have been rated to be the major problem followed by financial problems like use of resource and lack of costing systems, marketing, entrepreneurial inadequacy, lack of systems, bad quality of products and inventory built up in that order.

(b) Real Management Consultancy Needs of SSIs

Project consultation is the most important management consultancy need of SSIs during pre-production period followed by market development, financial services like cost reduction, training to the owner and his staff, suggestions for quality controls and rationalisation of inventories etc. during post-production period.

(c) Reasons for low utilisation of management consultancy services by SSIs

Lack of awareness in the SSI entrepreneurs about the benefits of consultants and their existence, high cost of service and lack of expertise for SSI units to be the major reasons for not serving SSI units. It may also mean that these are the reasons for not availing management consultancy services by the SSI units during post-production period.

(d) Suggestions for improving the utilisation of management consultancy services by SSIs

Developing awareness about importance of management

consultancy services for SSI units, marketing of the services, reducing the cost of services, improving commitment of the SSI entrepreneurs in the growth of their units,. improving the quality of consultancy service and understanding their real management problems can improve the utilisation of management consultancy services by SSI units during the post production period.

7.1.4.2 *The user group*

(a) Management Problems of SSIs

Marketing and financial management problems are the main areas of concern for the SSI units followed by personnel, production and project management in that order respectively.

(b) Real Management Consultancy Needs of SSIs

Marketing, finance, personnel, production and general management as major areas of consultation in that order of preference.

(c) Reasons for low utilisation of management consultancy services by SSIs

Bad quality of service, high cost of service, lack of awareness amongst SSI entrepreneurs about the role and benefits of management consultancy services, inflexible approach of consultants regarding fee etc., inability of SSI entrepreneurs to identify their real management/technical problems and absence of any compulsion to hire consultants during post production period unlike pre-production period for taking financial and other benefits are major reasons for lower utilisation of management consultants by SSI units.

(d) Suggestions for improving the utilisation of management consultancy services by SSIs

Utilisation of management consultancy services by SSI units during post production period can be improved provided the quality of service in improved, cost of service is reduced and services are marketed properly.

7.1.5 Perception Gaps

The perceptions of various interest groups which were approached by the researcher have been compared and the gaps in the perception is presented below.

1. With regards to the internal problems of the SSI units, the user groups feels that marketing is the main problem but the consultants feel that sub optimal use of resource is the main problem. There is no disputes about the importance of pre-production mistakes.
2. On the consultancy needs also the perception of the SSI units and the consultants vary. The SSI units rate marketing as the most important area of consultation but the consultants rate finance including optimal use of resources as the most important consultancy need.
3. There is no gap in the pattern of internal management problems and the management consultancy needs.
4. The supply of the management consultancy services is not as per the demand and there is wide gap for the post production period. The marketing and financial services are the key requirements but their supply is quite low. Therefore this is second type of gap in the supply in reference to demand in addition to the problem of geographical location already highlighted above.
5. There is gap in the perception of the users and the supplier group with regards to the reasons for low utilisation of the consultancy services by the SSI units during post production period. User group feels that non availability of competent consultants and high cost of service are main reasons followed by lack of awareness but the supplier group places whole emphasis on lack of awareness followed by

cost of service and gives least importance to the quality of service.

6. The main concerns of the consultants while consulting with SSI units are lack of awareness in the SSI entrepreneurs about the benefits of management consultancy services and the payment problem they face with them whereas the user SSI units are more concerned about the quality of service and its cost. Thus there is a clear gap in the perception of the supplier and the users of management consultancy services.
7. The majority of SSI units prefer lump sum payment system which can be bargained in the beginning but the majority of consultants report system of consultants man days being followed by them for estimating and charging fee. Thus there is gap in what the customer (SSI units) prefer and what he has to follow.
8. The majority of SSI units want long term association of the consultants through retainer consultancy whereas majority of consultants prefer engagement on assignment basis. Here also there is gap in the users preference and the supplier's practice.
9. There is no gap in the extent of use of consultants by the SSI units and the extent of service to this sector by the consultants.
10. Most of the consultants are in the private sector and most of the consultants whose services were availed by the SSI units were also in private sector.
11. 90% of the SSI respondents were aware about the benefits of management consultancy services but the consultants and their association were of the view that most of the SSI entrepreneurs are not aware about the benefits of the management consultancy services. Thus there is gap in this respect. However considering the fact that the

sample is urban based, the level of ignorance may increase in regard to SSI entrepreneurs located in the semi-urban and rural areas.

12. The clients (SSI units) their associations and the financial institutions do not think that the available services are useful for SSI sector and they place emphasis on improving the quality of services and reducing the cost but the consultants do not accept it and place more emphasis on the awareness problem. Thus there is wide gap in the perception of the suppliers and the users .
13. With regards to the steps to be taken to improve the use of management consultancy services by the SSI units during post production period, there is wide gap in the perception of the users and the suppliers. Supplier group place emphasis on improving the awareness of the SSI entrepreneurs about the utility of management consultancy services whereas he user group emphasises improvements in quality of service and reduction in the cost of service followed by improvements in the level of awareness of SSI entrepreneurs.

7.2 INFERENCES OF THE STUDY

On the basis of conclusions drawn in the preceding paragraph, the following inferences can be drawn for the purpose of furthering the present level of knowledge about the quality of management consultancy services for small scale industrial units in India as well formulating recommendations which may be implemented by SSI units, Management Consultants desirous of serving SSI units, their trade associations and government and other developmental agencies interested in the development of SSI sector and management consultancy profession.

1. There is geographical gap in the demand and supply

of management consultancy services for SSI units.

2. Private sector dominates the consultancy profession, soleproprietership and partnership firms dominating the scene and the size being very small leaving lesser chances of organisational complexity.
3. Majority of the consultants are professionally qualified and possess reasonable length of experience.
4. Part time consultants are utilised by majority of firms to take care of fluctuations in demand for different types of services.
5. Consultancy profession is presently dominated by technocrats having no in-depth knowledge of management tools and techniques as well as experience of management consultation.
6. Project/industrial consultancy is widely utilised for establishing new units, expansion, modernisation and rehabilitation of sick units but basically for availing financial/other benefits.
7. Utilisation of management consultancy services by SSI during post production period for solving managerial problems is very low, the areas of consultation being general management, personnel, production, marketing and finance in that order of importance.
8. Consultant man days consumed is the dominant method of estimating and charging consultancy fee, the assignment basis being the major mode of engagement.
9. In-house management expertise is mostly missing from the SSI sector as a whole.
10. Majority of the SSI entrepreneurs are not satisfied with the present level of the performance of their units.
11. Majority of the SSI entrepreneurs have faith in the

role of management tools and techniques as well as the management consultants in improving their performance.

12. Majority of the SSI units do not utilise the services of management consultants for solving post production management problems.
13. Majority of the SSI entrepreneurs prefer retainer consultancy with lump sum payments which is not popular as yet.
14. Recommendation of the consultants are not implemented due to their impracticability.
15. Majority of the SSI units were not satisfied with the quality of services availed in the past. Therefore the quality of service is not considered to be good.
16. In most of the cases no proper diagnostic analysis was conducted by SSI units before hiring consultants and they were hired in an ad hoc manner.
17. Intention to professionalise is hardly visible in the SSI units.
18. The expectations of the parties were not clear in most of the post production assignments, consultancy contracts either missing totally or having vague terms and conditions.
19. Marketing, finance and then personnel are the most important management problems before the SSI units which they may like to solve may be with outside help.
20. At the initial stage the project management services remain critical but after the production has commenced the marketing services will become the most important service required by the SSI units followed by financial services including cost reduction and working capital management, optimal use of resources and the personnel services

including training to the entrepreneurs and their staff.

21. Inadequate quality of service, high cost, mistrust between the SSI units and the consultants, lack of awareness in the SSI units about the benefits of consultancy service in improving the performance of the SSI units and lack of interest of the entrepreneurs in growth of their units, are the main reasons of low utilisation of the consultancy services by the SSI units in the post production period.
22. The major short comings in project consultancy services being supply of all data related to technical and marketing aspects to the consultants by the SSI units themselves, theoretical project estimates, failure of the consultants in convincing the bankers about the amount of loan required, bureaucratic approach of the Govt./public sector consultants and lack of practical inputs in the training programmes arranged by them during post production period and delay in completing the assignment.
23. The perception of the management consultants about the management problems of SSIs, their real management consultancy needs, reasons for low utilisation of management consultancy services during post production management problems, system of payments, modes of engagement, awareness of SSI about the benefits of the management consultancy services for SSI units and finally their suggestions for improving the utilisation of management consultancy services by SSI units does not match with the perception of SSI units. This gap indicates the basic reason behind the level of dissatisfaction amongst the SSI units with the quality of services availed by them in the past.

24. The quality of consultancy service can be improved by in-depth training of the consultants about the practical aspects of SSI working, their empenelment after proper screening, gaining experience about SSIs working, dependability and commitment for the development of their clients, providing simple and practical suggestions and providing flexible consultancy packages with flexible cost of service.
25. A viable marketing strategy has to include all steps such as creation of awareness in the clients through seminars/brain storming sessions with the SSI units and their associations, proper training to the entrepreneurs and their staff in identification of their real problems, need for a professional approach, usefulness of management consultants, their selection and use and how to maintain a healthy relationship, enlistment of consultant with all the bodies such as industry associations, state directorate of industries, DICs, financial institutions, industrial development authorities and SISI etc., taking help of branch managers of the commercial banks, direct selling using past references, developing and marketing prototype consultancy services on cheaper cost and going for retainer consultancy. The small business consultants could establish their institute or association if IMCI fails to meet their expectations.
26. The cost of service could be reduced through retainer consultancy with 4 or 5 SSI units, solo practice without any overhead, use of retired persons as consultants, use of prototype services, govt. subsidy, paperless and cheap consultation methods and use of less qualified persons as bare foot consultant working under the supervision of expert available on the regional level.

7.3 RECOMMENDATIONS

It has been reaffirmed by this study that majority of SSI units are not satisfied with the present level of their performance and do not utilise the management consultancy services to the extent desirable due to bad quality of these services and high cost. However they have faith in the efficacy of management tools and techniques as well as the role of management consultants in solving their problems and improving their performance. Therefore the future of management consultancy profession appears to be bright. However number of problems have surfaced in this study. Therefore taking into account the results of this study as inferred in the preceding section, the following recommendations are being forwarded for consideration and implementation by concerned parties.

1. At present the management consultants are only available in the metros and other important cities and the quality of their services is also not acceptable to the SSI units. Therefore it is essential to develop competent management consultants having multiple skills in the areas of technology, management and law especially suited to the needs of the SSI sector through out the country both in the urban and rural areas. This may be done by picking up the existing technical and management consultants as well as suitable technical personnel preferably diploma holders with some working experience of SSI sector (may be 10 years) and training them thoroughly in the SSI working, special nature of their management styles and problems and how to give them paper less advice in a simple way which is easier for them to implement without much of a financial strain. This could be done by management consultants associations, Govt., TCOs, SISIs Productivity Councils etc. may be with the help of some reputed private consultants.

2. A country like Japan was having about 35000 small business consultants in the year 1984 whereas India with about 3 millions SSI units has only around 15000 consultants majority of whom do not serve SSI sector due to various reasons highlighted in this study. Even if it is assumed that one small business consultant can effectively serve 10 clients on retainership basis (A mode preferred by majority of the SSI clients) and 75% of the SSI units are not satisfied with their present performance level, we require over 200,000 consultants only to serve the small scale sector. Therefore the task of training and developing such a large force is very challenging. Therefore Govt. (planning commission) should come forward and plan it out may be through agencies like SIDBI. This will not only give added impetus to the growth of SSI sector but also open a new avenue of self employment for the energetic, creative and hard working persons. Therefore this programme should be made a corner stone of the industrial development policy of the states and central Govt.
3. Continuous development of consultants capabilities as well as effective control of service quality is essential for healthy growth of consultancy profession for small scale sector. Therefore small business consultants could establish their separate institute if the IMCI does not cater to their needs. The consultancy for small and large industrial units are two entirely separate area quite different from each other.
4. As SSI units can not afford different consultants for different needs, small scale sector requires technical, management and legal services under one roof. Therefore training has to take care of this requirement.

5. The consultancy profession has to develop in the private sector to have full flexibility and responsiveness to the changing economic scenario and TCO's/SSI/DICs could only work as catalyst and be medium of necessary government support for this profession.
6. It is not essential that B.Tech./M.Tech. or MBAs serve as consultants to the SSI sector as the inputs given to them is not considered suitable to the special needs of the small scale sector. Therefore we may pick up diploma holders and train them in the management and law especially suited to the needs of small scale industries.
7. In order to meet the demand of this type of manpower, it is suggested that all Indian universities/colleges /polytechniques should start two years part time diploma course in small business consultancy. The course may include the technology for small enterprises, management concepts, theories and practices as applicable to small business, labour, factory and other industrial and mercantile laws as applicable to the small industry, project conception, financing and implementation. They can take help of enlightened entrepreneurs in designing course content and giving practical inputs to the participants as well as arranging their field training. It will be better to pick up technically qualified supervisors/foremen working with SSI units for more than 10 years and encourage them to join such courses on part time basis. Practicing consultants who wants to develop their consultancy skills may also join this course.
8. At present very few Indian universities/colleges offer courses on Entrepreneurship and small business as available in USA (more than 20 universities) and many more countries. It has been established that the SSI entrepreneurs are not aware

of the benefits of consultants' advice. Therefore it is suggested that all Indian universities and colleges should start two years part time morning/evening diploma course in entrepreneurship and small industry management. The course besides having other inputs, should also have input on the consultancy services and should include aspects such as benefits of consultants, how to select and use consultants and viability problems of the consultancy firms. This could be utilised by entrepreneurs who want to improve their managerial effectiveness. Full time one year course could be planned for prospective entrepreneurs.

9. The ITIs/polytechniques/colleges could provide part-time one year course on small scale supervision and management for the supervisors/ foremen of SSI units. This should have basic management inputs suitable for SSI management. They could have full time course for prospective candidates seeking employment with SSI units as supervisors/ managers.
10. The culture of solo consultant is to be developed to reduce the cost of service to the SSI units.
11. Retired persons who have relevant qualification and experience could also work as small business consultants after proper training. This will reduce the cost of services as they may be financially stable.
12. The entrepreneurs who are doing well and have proper exposure may also work as consultants to small units who are not their direct or indirect competitors.
13. Less qualified (diploma holders) but experienced persons may work under an experienced expert available at the regional level and they may turn out to be cheaper.

14. The consultants should serve SSI units in a clusters to reduce the overhead costs.
15. The consultants should restrict engagement on assignment basis only for project consultation and should go for retainer consultation in all other cases to develop long term relations.
16. Monthly retainer fee may start from Rs 2500 and may go up to Rs 10000 or even more depending upon the paying capacity of the client.
17. As the prime consultancy needs of the SSI units during the post production period are marketing, financial and general management services, the consultants who wish to serve them should develop skills in the areas of market analysis and development, cost reduction, working capital management, optimal use of resources, training to the entrepreneurs and their staff. A lot of emphasis is to be placed on tools of financial analysis.
18. The consultants should charge fee on lump sum basis followed by other methods such as % of profits or sales in place of present system of charging on the basis of consultants man days.
19. The consultants should develop trustworthiness, dependability and full commitment towards the all round growth of their clients and also for protecting the public funds invested in the client's firms. The organisations enlisting the consultants should screen them thoroughly for these attributes with the help of psychological tests.
20. Consultants must provide simple and practical suggestions keeping in view the educational level of the entrepreneur and the status of his unit.
21. They should develop prototype consultancy packages and market them to reduce the cost of service.

22. The consultants could adopt flexible approach in respect of consultancy fee. They should ask fee taking into account the financial position of the firm and the likely benefits of their services .This should be treated as investment in future .
23. The awareness of the entrepreneurs about the likely benefits of the consultancy service should be increased through seminars/brain storming sessions with the entrepreneurs at the industrial estates with the help of their associations. The IMCI should prepare a general publicity material on the likely benefits of the consultancy services and should be distributed at such seminars or on other important occasions. IMCI may create special fund for this purpose by taking contributions from the small business consultants.
24. The consultants should enlist themselves with the industry associations, IMCI, DICs state directorate of industries, financial institutions, industrial development authorities who may further circulate the list to their branches.
25. However proper screening of the small business consultants is a must for ensuring that only competent consultants are available on the list. The Consultancy Development Center New Delhi may create some sort of independent ratings for small business consultants after psychological and professional tests. This could be used by other agencies for enlisting the consultants. Japan has very tough screening process for registering the consultants even for small and medium enterprises and similar methods could be followed in India also.
26. Like the courses suggested above for universities etc. the entrepreneurial development programmes (EDPs) being run by the state govt., SISIs, TCOs,

banks etc. should include a capsule on small business consultancy. This should include inputs connected with diagnosis of problems, selection and use of consultant and their viability problems.

27. The branch managers of the commercial banks should be properly trained in the area of small business consultancy, so as to work as effective liaison man between the consultants and the clients. Thus vast rural/urban network of banks could be utilised for this purpose. This could be in the interest of banks.
28. The financial institutions should develop an early warning system, so as to detect problematic industrial units at early stage, so that they could be asked to seek the assistance of consultant at early stage and improve rather than waiting till the unit becomes sick and rehabilitation becomes very difficult .
29. The Reserve Bank of India should enforce a condition in the loan agreements regarding engagement of consultants in case a unit fails to repay the loan continuously as per schedule for some specified period.
30. The consultants should first approach and work for units having professional owners to their satisfaction and then obtain reference from them. Thereafter they should approach new clients with past track record and references and resort to direct selling.
31. The consultancy fee could be partly linked with the results i.e. increase in sales/profit or decrease in loss, the benefit being at least double the consultancy fee. Though as per the code of conduct the consultants are not allowed to claim such benefits but their past records should speak for them.

32. The promoters contribution should not be less than 40% for his commitment towards the growth of his unit.
33. The owners should spell out their expectations from the consultants very clearly in the beginning itself by entering into consultancy contracts with clear terms and conditions to avoid any misunderstanding in the future.
34. The consultants should learn the regional languages/dialects for effective communication with the client and his people.
35. Consultants should be able to suggest cost reduction after a quick study.
36. In case of retainership consultant should visit the client once in a week but should be available on telephone on other working days also.
37. Government should consider management audit compulsory for all the units who have borrowed public fund, like financial audit.

7.4 RECOMMENDATIONS FOR FURTHER RESEARCH

This is the first academic study on this subject in India and is based on urban oriented samples. Therefore, in order to more throw light on the subject from different angles, the following further studies are being recommended.

1. Similar study may be conducted by taking a sample of the SSI units located in rural areas to highlight their requirements. However to keep the cost within limits few local samples could be utilised.
2. Few selected case studies of small business consultation may be conducted in detail to identify the specific problem areas.
3. We could compare the consultancy practices of Indian consultants with the consultants working

in developed countries like Japan, U.S.A, U.K and Canada.

4. Studies may be conducted separately for other market segments/customer groups such as corporate, public and govt. sectors and voluntary organisations.
5. Studies may be conducted for specific segments of consultancy industry such as TCOs, SISIs, productivity councils and private consultants.
6. A study may be conducted to assess the impact of the policies of related institutions, such as term lending institutions, commercial banks, district industry centers and industry associations on the growth of consultancy culture in India.
7. A similar study may be conducted to compare the prevalent consultancy practices in India with those available in the other developing countries having similar socio-economic conditions.
8. A comparative study may be conducted to assess the role of government in fostering the consultancy culture in various countries .
9. Comparative studies may also be done separately for other agencies like financial institutions and associations of industries and consultants.
10. The study indicated in the preceding para may be done for developed as well as developing countries.
11. The functioning of District Industry Centres in promoting excellent in the management of Small Scale Industries can be studied.

Bibliography

Accountant, Providing advice and financial supports- 99; 143 Jan. 1987

Advani R.H., Indian management consultancy—emerging trends, *Business India,* Oct 1989 pp. 16-19

Agrawal P. N., Learning from the Japanese—Small and medium industries, *Indian Management* Dec 1987

Agrawal Vijay, Information technology for management consultancy: opportunities, issues, and training, (IM) Jan.1989, 28 (1)

Allen R. Kohen, Goden Herman and Fink Stephen, Key groups and not T- group for O.D, *Consultants and consultancy styles* Edited by Dharni P. Sinha, Vision Books 1979 p. 248

Ansari Nazir Ahmad, *Management techniques of small scale and cottage industries with special reference to Benaras Handloom Industry* Ph. D. Thesis 1958 AMU

Arnold Putman, Challenge to the profession, *Journal of Management Consultancy* (JMC) 5(2) pp. 14-19

Axton L.L., Hiring a consultant? First do your home work, *Personnel* 58(6) Nov.-Dec. 1981 pp. 39-43

Azad R.R, Arora Usha, Financial constraints of small scale sector, *Yojna* 32(4)

Badekar S.S, Development of comprehensive consultancy services for small and medium scale enterprises Management consultancy Development Phase I (small enterprises), Final report by Management Development Institute Gurgoan, India (hereafter referred as MCDPI)

Bansal Anand and Gupta R.C., Management Consultancy - need for regulation, (*IM*) Jan. 1989, 28(1) pp.16-21

Basu S. K, *Plan and problems of small industries*, Mukharjee and Co. Pvt. Ltd. 1957

Basu S.K., *Problems and possibilities of ancillary industries in a developing economy—Survey of ancillary units in West Bengal*, World Press, 1965

Bauer P.T., *Determinants of development- An dissent on development*, Weidenfield and Nicolson, London, 1976

Beckhard Richard, Organisational changes through consultation and training, *Consultants and Consultancy Styles*, Edited by Dharni P. Sinha, Vision Books 1979, p. 248

Berry M.L., Management consultancy—A user's view point, *Administrator* Vol. 28(3 and 4)1963

Berry J., Consultants wake up to human resources, *Human Resource Management* 22(3) 1983 Fall pp. 287-296.

Bhatta U.V. Financial Institutions and TCOs—The Indian experience in small enterprises promotion, *Vikas Banking* 1992

Bhattacharya A.B., Indian management- Present trends and future needs, *Indian Industries*, vol. ix no. 7 July 1965 37-40

Bhattacharya S.K, Consultancy as a tool of management development, role of business schools, *Economic and Political Weekly* 12(35)

Bhusan B.S.N, Are professional management services compatible with the present day requirements of modern day trade and industries, Industrial conference on corporate management and investment, 8th June 1968

Bianco V.E., The internal consultant and the eternal struggle, *Training and Development Journal*, 39, July 1985 pp. 51-53

Bidani S.N. and Mishra P. K., *Industrial sickness — Identification and Rehabilitation*, Vision Books 1982

Bird J, Choosing a consultant, *Management Today*, June 1992 pp. 86-87

Blake Robert R Every and Manton Jane Srygley, Manager as

OD consultant, *Consultants and consultancy styles* Edited by Dharni P. Sinha, Vision Books, 1979, p. 248

Bloom Franlin B., Managing on going fee relationship, (*JMC*) 7(1)1991

Bloom Paul N., Effective marketing for professional firms, *HBR* Sept- Oct. 1984

Blustain Harvey, Consultant as shamans, *Journal of Management Consultancy* 7(1) 1992 Spring

Braker J.S. and Pearson J.N., The impact of consultants on small firms strategy planning, *Journal of Small Business Management* 23, 23-30 July 1985

Brocknan W. L., Prospects for malpractices suits in business consulting profession, *Journal of Business* 50(1) Jan. 1977 pp. 70-73

Brook Michael J., Effective use of consultants, *Management Accounting* 59(4) April 1981 pp. 39-40

Brook Michael J., What do consultants do? *Management Accounting* 58(8) Sept 1980 pp. 33-38

Burke Warner W., One consultant's trip from technique to theory, *Consultants and consultancy styles*, Dharni P. Sinha (ed.), Vision Books 1979 p. 248

Business America, Management Consultancy services continue rapid growth overseas, 1985, 014, pp. 813-814

Calvest Markhan, *Top consultants developing your skills for grater effectiveness*

Cash William B. and Minter Robert L., Consulting approaches— two basic styles, *Training and Development Journal* 33(9) Sept 1979 pp. 26-28

Chakravorty S.N., Management consultancy services and use of computers, *Management Accountant* 18(1) Jan 1983 pp. 23-24

Chatterjee P., Impediments to higher productivity in small industries, *Indian Management* vol. 3 no 6 Nov.-Dec. 1964 pp. 38-42

Chattopadhyaya P., Consultancy for small business, *Financial Express*, 7th Feb. 1990 p. 7

Chaudhary, K.V.R. and Reddy B.V.K, Success in rural small Entrepreneurship, *Indian Management* Feb 1981

Churchill Neil C. and Lewis Verinia L, Five stages of small business growth, *Harvard Business Review,* May -June 1983 pp. 30- 43

Cohen W.A., *Counsel for consultant*

Conner J.V.O., Discrete capability factor in marketing professional services, *Industrial Marketing Management,* Oct 1978 Vol. 7(5)

Corin T.J. and Fisher T.K., Consultant and client must work together (*JMC*) 6(4)1990 pp. 11-19

Coxe Weld, For professionals the bottom line is not always the bottom line, *Journal of Management Consultancy* 7(1) 1992 Spring pp. 35-40

Curisman J.J., Impact of SBDC consulting activities, *Journal of Small Business Management* 23,1-11, July 1985

Dasgupta A., Management consultancy in India, *Times of India,* 14th March1989 p.13.1

Dayal, Iswar, The consultant and his style, Dharni P. Sinha (ed.), *Consultants and consultancy styles,* Vision Books 1979, p. 248

Dharwadkar, P.P., Consultancy Exports- 8th plan perspectives, *Economic Times* 28th Sept. 1989 p. 7

Desponde Manohar U., *Entrepreneurship of small scale industries,* Deep and Deep Publications New Delhi, 1989

Devid S.E., My consulting style, Consultants and consultancy styles Edited by Dharni P. Sinha, Vision Books 1979 p. 248

Dharni P. Sinha, Consulting for OD, *Consultants and consultancy styles,* Dharni P. Sinha (ed.), Vision Books 1979 p. 248

Dixit B.K., Small scale industries—Ills and remedies, *Yojna* 32(4)

Duncan Ian, Generating Ideas: explorers and artists wanted, *The Management Accounting,* vol. 66 no. 3 April 1992

Dunn Donald H., *Before you hand out—A consultant's struggle: Nation's Business* no. 87

Economic Times (Editorial), Indian consultancy, 22nd April 1989

Economic Times (Editorial) Exports of consultancy services, 1st Feb. 1986 p. 5

Economic Times (Editorial), Time to strengthen consultancy units, 24th March 1988

Economist, Consultants need to manage themselves—304 Sept. 12 1987 pp. 71-79

Economist, Management Consultancy- The new witch doctor, 306 Feb. 13,1988 p. 3

Economist, Solution Peddlers lose their charms, vol. 318, 1991

Eibis William J., A better way to pick a consultant, *Journal of Management Consultancy*, 2(4) 1985

Elotraff J.B., Procedure for improving the evaluation of SBDC consultation activities, *Journal of Small Business Management*, 25, pp. 67-71

Feller, Sherley J. and Frandsen Steen B., Have we been our own worst enemy? *JMC*, Vol. 7(3) 1993

Ford John Black, Consulting for the small companies, *Journal of Management Consultancy*, 7(2) 1992 Fall pp. 25-28

Freeman Devid M., Tailored services for small firms. *Nation's Business* No. 74 April 1986 pp. 22-24

Furnham Adrian, The academic consultant—*Journal of general management*, Vol. 7(2) winter 1991 pp. 13-19

Gauguly Nirmal, Small scale sector-problems and prospects, *Yojna* 32(4)

George Baldwin B., Industrial growth in south India—case studies in economic development, Free Press, 1959

Glanser Michel J and Axley Stephan R, Consulting activities of university faculty members - scope and depth of involvement - *Group and Organisational Studies* 8(3) Sept.1983 pp. 270-284

Glassman Alom M., Laund Berg and Craig O.J., In search of a right consultant-An OD fable, *Group and Organisational Studies*, 13(1)March 1988 pp. 5-18

Golden Godfrey, Consultants specialising to services, *The Sunday Times*, 25th Aug. 1991, p. 49.

Golembiewski R.T., Some perspectives on one's consulting style, Dharni P. Sinha (ed.), *Consultants and Consultancy Styles*, Vision Books 1979 p. 248

Grant N.B., The management consultancy syndrome, *Indian Management*, July 1989 pp. 30-32

Gray Gonglas A., *Entrepreneur's complete Self-Assessment Guide*

Grriel Gelb M., Arm your consultancy practice with market research, *JMC*2(4) 1985

Guest Robert H., Challenges for the year 2001, *Journal of Management Consultancy*, 2(4) 1985

Gumpert D.E. and Boyd D. P., The loneliness of small business owner, *Harvard Business Review* Nov. Dec. 1984

Gupta Vidya Sagar, *Small scale Industry in India- An appraisal of its financing by SFCs and IDBI*, Ph.D. thesis BHU 1991

Hall W.P, Managing quality in consultancy - *JMC* 6(3) pp. 44-49

Hamilton Bratice E. and Smith Preston G., Implementing TQM on a shoe string, *Journal of Management Consultancy* 7(4) 1993 Fall

Harding Charle F., Rain making, JMC Vol. 7(1) 1992 pp. 59-63

Harigopal K. and Saikishar V, Small Enterprises- Sustaining and Enhancing growth potential, *Indian Management* 30(10-11) Nov. 1991 pp. 3-10

Harper Malcolm, *Consulting for small business- The concept and training for consultants*

Harvard Business Review, Consultancy services - how to use? Reprint no. 90039

Harvard Business School USA, *Management consultancy* 1989-90—a placement guide

Head William N. and Carson William M., Consulting to small Business in Australia, *Journal of Management Consultancy* 8(1) 1994 spring

Hjelhott Gunner, North to the Polar Circle, Dharni P. Sinha (ed.), *Consultants and consultancy styles,* Vision Books 1979 p. 248

Holtze Herman, *Utilising consultants effectively- A guide to management in business and Govt.*

Hosmer, Cooper and Vesper, *The Entrepreneurial function — Text and cases on small firms,* Prentice Hall Inc. New Jersey 1977

Hotch Riplay, *Franchising -Nation's Business* No. 73 Sept. 1985 pp. 37-38

Howard Robert, Can small business help countries compete, *Harvard Business Review* Nov.- Dec. 1990

Hubbon Herbert, Do consultants earn their kept?- *Across the Board,* June 1987, p. 6

Hughes, M., Establishment of a business information services in Coopers and Lybrand, Deloiltee, *The Intelligent Enterprise,* Jan. 1992 pp. 16-19

Human Relations, Systematic appraisal of leadership effectiveness of the consultants—36(11) Nov. 1983, pp. 1045-1064

Industrial Times, Management consultancy- A much maligned profession: battling for survival, June 19-July 2.

Jaganathan R., Is consultancy taking off, *Business World,* Feb 1989 pp. 29-31

Jain Hemchand, Small industries in India, *Industrial India,* Oct. 1969vol. 20no 10 pp. 41-47

Jacobson Ian C., Thinking of becoming an independent consultant? *JMC* 6(3) 1990 p. 22-25

Jacobson Ian C., What makes PPC succeed? *JMC* 6(1) pp. 24-28 1990.

Jakodia G.B, Management Consultancy- declining in small scale sector, *Laghu Udyog Samachar,* May 1984

Jani D. K., *Marketing management of SSIs,* Prateeksha Publications, Jaipur, 1988

Jay A., Rate yourself as a consultant, *HBR* 55(4) July-Aug 1977 pp. 84-92

Johson Sharon G., Consulting as marketing management, *Journal of Small Business Management* Vol. 19(4) Oct 1981 pp. 10-14

Joshi N.C., It does needs spoon feeding, *Yojna* 32(4)

Journal of General Management, The academic consultant, 17(2) Winter 1991 pp. 13-19

Journal of Management Consultancy, Incremental strategy for consultancy success vol. P(2) p. 8

Journal of Management Consultancy, Training for changing consultant's role 5(3)

Journal of Management Consultancy, Training and management of consultant, 7(1) 1992 Spring pp. 3-8

Journal of Management Consultancy, Unhappy clients—who is to be blamed? Vol. 6(4)1990

J.P.Frankenhus, How to get a good consultant? *HBR* 55(6) Nov.- Dec. 1977 pp. 133-139

Kaplan Roger, Entrepreneurship reconsidered -The anti management bias, *HBR* reprint no. 87304

Kellongg Diane Mckinnery, Contracting successful and unsuccessful OD consultative relationship, *Group and Organisational Studies* 9(2) June 1984 pp. 151-176

Khajuria R.M., Strategic role of management consultants in developing small industry sector- Paper presented at first Asia-Pacific conference on management consultancy held on May 23 to May 26 1989

Khan R.R., *Management of Small Scale Industries,* S. Chand and Co., Delhi 1979

Khanna R.W., Indian Management Services Exports from India - trends abroad and Indian affords, *Indian Management,* 28(1) Jan 1989 pp. 11-14

Khurana S.S, Industrial sickness in India, *Indian Management* Oct 1992

King Leslie, Advice from consultants: How they sell their ideas and how you should sell yours? *Industrial Eng.* Vol. 20(7)

Krishna Bharat, Strategic Planning - How consultancy helps, *IM* 28(1), Jan.1989 pp. 42-47

Krishnamoorthy N, Service sector in the 1990's- Management Issues *IM* 28(1) Jan. 1989

Kubr M.(Ed.), *Management Consultancy- A guide to the profession*, Third edition, ILO Genewa, 1996

Kumar V., India in transition - Role of management consultants, *IM* 31(5) Oct 92 pp. 36-38

Laghu Udyog Samachar, Measures to revive sick units, vol. 12 no. 7 Feb 1988

Lakadwala D.T., *Small industry in a big city—A survey in Bombay* 1960

Lakshman T. K, *Cottage and small scale industries in Mysore- A case study of their pattern and role in context of a developing economy*, Mysore, Rao and Raghavan 1966

Landlorio J. S, Confidentiality and consultant's agreement, *Journal of Management Consultancy*, 8(1) 1994 spring

Larwood Lauric and Gattiker Urs E., Client and consultant, management problems solving values, *Group and Orgaisational Studies* 11(4) Dec. 1986 pp. 374-386

Larwood Lauric and Gattiker Urs E., Rational bias and international power in the employment of management consultants, *Group and Organisatinal Studies*, vol. 10(1) March 1985 pp. 3-17

Lauenstein Milton C., Cutting companies to size, *Havard Business Review*, 84(5) Sept.-Oct. 1984

Lewin Richord and Travis Virginia R., Small company finance—what books do not say, *HBR* Nov. Dec. 1987 87(6)

Liebawitz Benard and Jay Goltz, When consultants are hired?

Journal of Management Consultancy 7(3) 1993 Spring pp. 11-14

Lippitt Gordon L., Changing role of a consultant -A case example, *Consultants and consultancy styles* Edited by Dharni P. Sinha, ed., Vision Books 1979 p. 248

Lippit Ronald, Dimensions of consultant's job, *The Journal of Social Issues,* 1959, vol. XV 5-12

Lorsch Jay W and Maithias Peter F, When professionals have to manage, *HBR* July-Aug 1987

Lundlerg Craig C., Transactions and Games in management consultancy, *Journal of Management Consultancy* 8(1) Spring 1994

Lyle William G. and Rates D.L., When do you hire a consultant? *Industrial Eng.* 11(6) Jan. 1979 pp. 34-37

Lyuton Rolf P. and Thomas John M., Utility of institution building theory for strategy and methodology for consultation, *Consultants and consultancy styles,* Dharni P. Sinha, Vision Books 1979 p. 248

Mahapatra A.K., Management consultancy for small industries *(MCDPI)*

Maheshwari B.L., *Consultant* as guru — expectations and experiences, *Consultants and consultancy styles,* Dharni P. Sinha, Vision Books 1979 p. 248

Main J., Under the spell of quality Guru -*Fortune* (international) 114(4) Aug. 18 1986, p. 24

Management Accounting (UK), Developing a consulting practice, 64(1) Jan 1986 pp. 18-20

Management Development Institute Gurgoan India, Management consultancy Development Phase I (small enterprises), *Final report* (MCDPI)

Manfred F. R.Kete de Vries, Dark side of Entrepreneurship, *Harvard Business Review* no. 6 Nov. Dec. 1985

Mann C.K., Grindle M .S. and Shipton P. : *Seeking solution, Frame work and cases for small enterprises Development Programme,* Kumaria Press Inc. 1980 p. 434

Mazim A.C., Seasons of consultant's life, *Training and Development Journal,* 39(9) Sept 1985 pp. 47-52

Medonald Edwin D., Plumbers and Philosophers : Service value and need *(JMC)* 6(1) 1990 pp. 4-8

Menon K.R.N., A new concept in consultancy, *Industrial Times*

Metzer R.O., With so many consultants why are not we better? *Journal of Management Consultancy* vol. 5(3) p. 9-13

Miller Ernest C., When consultant needs a consultant—*Journal of Management Consultancy (JMC)* 5(1) 1989 pp. 43-46

Mishra P. K., *Industrial sickness- Role of entrepreneur,* Anmol Publications, New Delhi 1971

Mohindra Naresh, Strategic paper for a technical consultancy organisation, Prabandh April -Sept. 1992 pp. 15-17

Moldenhauer Charle A., How to sell consultancy services, *Journal of Small Business Management* Vol. 20(2) April 1982

Mauthoux D.C., Pierre Guiltel D. E., Marketing management consultant, *Industrial Marketing Management,* Vol. 7(2) April 1978 pp. 139-144

Mushkat Miron, Planning and Bureaucrats - Development of consultant- client relationships, *Long Range Planning* 17(2), April 1987 pp. 111-116

Nath Surendra, *Kuteer Udyog ki samasyayee avam sambhavanayaee - Charaee Gaon Vikas khand ka adhayan,* Ph.D. Thesis 1985 BHU

National Planning Commission, *Rural and Cottage Industries,* Bombay, Vora and Co.

National Productivity Council, New Delhi, *Management Consultancy capabilities in India* for Dept. of Scientific and Industrial Research Ministry of Science and Technology, Govt. of India, 1990.

Nelton Shavod, Campus connection for family business, *Nation's Business* no 76 Oct.1988

Nelton Shavod, Family business a hot market, *Nation's Business* no. 76 Oct 1988 pp. 22-34

Norris Devid B., To be or not to be a partner, *Journal of Management Consultancy* 7(3) Sept. 1993 Spring pp. 46-51

Nudd Devid, Management audit -A new approach, *Management Services*, vol. 30 no 10 1986

Ommen M. A., Anatomy of Entrepreneurship- A case study of Kerala, *Business Herald*, June 1969 vol. ii no 6

Panda P. K. and Mehar R. K., Industrial sickness—A case study of small scale industries, Ashis Publishing House, New Delhi 1992

Parikh Udai, Some Ethinoanto biographical notes on consulting, Consultants and consultancy styles Edited by Dharni P. Sinha, ed., Vision Books 1979 p. 248

Parmar Renu Singh, *Industrial sickness in small scale sector in India—A case study*. Ph.D. Thesis, BHU Commerce 1993

Pathak U.V., Relevance of Japanese management styles to Indian small business, *Indian Management*, 30(4-5), April May 1991 pp. 70-73

Payne A., New trends in strategy consultancy industry - Journal of business strategy 7(1) 1986 Summer pp. 43-45

Payne A. and Lumisdon C., Strategy consultancy—A shooting star, *Long Range Planning* 20(53-54) June 1987

Patnayak P.C., Perception of NEITCO in providing Management consultancy to small and medium industries (MCDPI)

Pech Richards J. and Alistair Mathew, Critical factors for consultancy to small business, *Journal of Management Consultancy*, 7(3) Spring 1993 pp. 61-63

Peterson R.A. and Kerin R.A., Effective use of market research consultants, *Industrial Marketing Management* 9 (69-71) 1980

Pick Pedro J., Relationship: the critical success factor in a management consultancy practice, *Journal of Management Consultancy*, 7(2) 1992 Fall pp. 3-5

Planning Commission, Govt. of India, Management consultancy needs for turn- around of SSIs—A study conducted by Management Development Institute Gurgaon, India, 1994

Poorman Stephen P., Turn- around consultancy is not in a recession: *Journal of Management Consultancy*, 7(3) Spring 1993 pp. 22-25

Price Charltron R. and Johari Hari P. Management consultancy in the global economy, *Journal of Management Consultancy* 7(2) 1992 Fall pp. 42-47

Raghavan S, How to develop in house management consultancy services, *MDI Journal of Management,* vol. (1 and 2) July 1985

Raghunathan N., SSI sector has long way to go, *Yojna* March,1-15 1988 vol. 32 (4)

Raju P.N.L., Growth with efficiency—the role of management consultancy in small scale industry in India, *SEDME* (1991) 18(1) 41-56

Raju P.S., Consultancy Support Services to small and medium enterprises, *Indian Management* May 1990 .

Rangachari J., Technical consultancy for power plants, (*IM*)28(1)

Rangnekar Sharu S., Get the best from your consultant- The client's role, *Indian Management* 28(12) Dec. 1989, pp. 9-11

Rangnekar Sharu S., Industrial sickness-causes and remedies, *Excellence in Supervision,* vol. 9 no. 3 May-June 1993

Rao R. V., *Cottage and small scale industries in a planned economy,* Jallandhar Sterling Publications 1967 p. 198

Rao Umamaheshswar Chandra, Management problems of SSI, *Indian Journal of Commerce* March-June 1959

Rastriya Sahara—Profile of sickness in 1991-92

Ratna Lalit K., Role and development of management consultancy in India, *Ambit* Oct 1978

Revell R.J., Local govt.- A challenge to management services, *Management Services,* Aug. 1980 vol 24 no. 5

Riech Robert B., Entrepreneurship reconsidered-The team as hero *HBR* reprint no. 87309

R. Kanh, Should marked up expenses be debited to client? (*JMC*) 6(3) 1990 pp. 11-13

Robonson Diana Gaine and Young L.B., To leap or slide: Transition from internal to external consultant, *Training and Development Journal,* 38(5) May 1984 pp. 40-46

Rohlen Thomson, Why Japanese education work? *HBR* Sept Oct 1987

Sadhak H., Role of TCOs in management consultancy in India, *Lok Udyog* April 1985

Saxena K.K., Industrial sickness in SSI sector—A perspective, *Southern Economist,* vol. 23 no. 24 April 1985

Schumacher E. F., *Small is beautiful,* Rupa and Co. 1990

SEDME, *Cases on management consultancy for small enterprises,* March 1986

Sekhar Ghose, Shake up and the fix it business, *Business Today* 1992 May 22-June 6

Sharma R. and Bajpai Shailendra, Financial ratios and identification of sickness in small scale sector : A view point, *Prabandh,* April-Sept. 1992 pp. 33-36

Sharma S.V.S., *Small entrepreneurial development in some Asian Countries—A comprehensive study,* Light and Life Publication, New Delhi 1979

Shay Michael E, How to avoid polluting market material or write a brochure that works, *JMC* 6(3) pp. 14-18

Shetty M.C., Entrepreneurship in small industry, *The Economic Weekly,* vol. 16 No. 22 May 1964

Shetty M. C., *Small scale and household industries in a developing economy—A study of their relations, structure and operative conditions,* Bombay, Asia Publishing House

Shukla Ashok, *Entrepreneurship and Innovation—A case study of selected SSI units of Varanasi,* Ph.D. thesis BHU 1989

Simson G.A., Clients measure you by ROI, (*JMC*) 6(1) 1990

Singh Birendra Narayan, Industrial Enterprises in U.P.—A case study of light engg units in KAVAL towns 1961 Ph.D. Thesis BHU

Singh Nirmal, Consulting in India -An overview, (*IM*) 28(1) Jan. 1989

Singh Nirmal, Guest editorial on management consultancy, *Indian Management* (*IM*)28(1) Jan. 1989 pp. 4-5

Singh Prithpal, The small scale and issue of management, *Indian Management* 29 (11,12) pp. 32-37

SISI Banglore, Management consultancy for SSIs (MCDPI)

SISI Bombay, Management consultancy and small units (MCDPI)

Small Industry Development Organisation, New Delhi, Techno -managerial consultancy scheme for north east, (MCDPI),

Smith Brian P., Marketing management consultancy, *JMC* 6(1) pp. 34-40

Srinivasan G., It is crucial for development, *Yojna* 32(4)

Sriram K.S., Quality in Small scale sector, *Productivity* Jan - March 1987

Srivastav S. P., IDBI and small units, *Yojna* 32(4)

Stevension Howard H. and Sahlman William A., How small comanies should handle advisors, *Harvard Business Review*, March-April 1988

Stevenson H.H. and Sahlman W.A, How small companies should handle consultants? *HBR* vol. 66 March -April 1988 pp. 28-34

Stuller J., When crisis doctor calls? *Across the Board*, May 1986, p. 45

Sundaram. V.M., Management consultancy and MIS-squaring the triangle, (*IM*) 28(1) Jan 1989 pp. 6-10 and 15

Suryanarayanan Shankar, Trends and outlook for U.S. consultancy—*JMC* 5(4).

Taneja Satish, Entrepreneurship and management, *Laghu Udyog Samachar* Nov. 1990 pp. 9-10

Taub Richard P. and Daub Doris L., Entrepreneurship in India's small scale industries, Mohan Publications 1989

Taveggia Thomos, Billing rates, *Journal of Management Consultancy* 7(2) 1992 Fall pp. 58-60

Teneyck R.C., Building sound client relationships: one consultant's experience, *JMC* 5(1) pp. 28-32

Tilles Seymour, Understanding consultant's role, *HBR* reprint no. 61608

Tindley Devis, Quality and management consultancy, Journal *of Management Consultancy* 7(2) 1992 Fall pp. 21-24

Tiwari D.N., *Entrepreneurial profiles and organisation structure of ancillary units in U.P.- A case study,* Ph.D. Thesis BHU 1989

T. Moline, Upgrading a consultant- (JMC) 6(2) 1990 pp. 17-22

Toor N. S., Financing SSIs—need for new approach, *Indian Banking Today and Tomorrow,* Aug 1993

Turner A.N., Consulting is more than giving advice, *HBR* 60(5) Sept.-Oct. 1982 pp. 120-129

Udyog Byapar Samachar. Nov. 1984 12(5), Co+tage and Village industries in Japan

Varadan S. S., Better Management of service sector, (*IM*) 28(1) Jan. 1989 pp. 3-6

Vepa Ram K., *Modern Small Scale Industry in India-Problems and prospects,* Sage Publications, New Delhi 1988

Wally B.H., Management services- A return to the relevance, *Management Services,* vol. 28 no. 2 Feb 1984

Warrior S.K., The success syndrome—Profiles of successful managers, *Indian Management* vol. 21 no. 2

Washburn Stewart A, Methodical selling works best, *JMC* 6(3)

Weihrich Heinz, Management practices in US, Japan and China, *Industrial Management,* March-April 1990, pp. 2-7

Weises S.A., How small companies should handle consultants? *HBR* Vol. no. 66

Weiss Allen, Preventing your job from getting in the way of your career, *Journal of Management Consultancy* 7(2) 1992 Fall pp. 36-38

William Hanld, Planning for productivity, *Management Service* Sept 1990 vol. 24

Yadav P.K. and Raj Kamal, Industrial sickness—The unforeseen reasons—A case study. *The Indian Journal of Commerce* Vol. XLVI part III No 176 Sept. 1993

Zvonimirradic, Consultancy in the model of contemporary technological development in the world, *IM* Jan. 1989, 28(1)

Appendices

APPENDIX-A

QUESTIONNAIRE FOR MANAGEMENT CONSULTANTS

(1) Please furnish following details about the status of your unit.

(a) Name and address ______________________

____

(b) Year of establishment______________________

(c) Constitution______________________

(d) Annual turn over (Rs in lakhs)______________

(e) Name, academic /professional qualifications and experience of the promoter/managing partner/ managing director ______________

(f) No. of consultants engaged

(i) Full time__________(ii) Part time __________

(g) Nos. of consultants with qualifications (I) MBA____(ii)MBA with Engg.______

(h) Nos. of consultants with experience of

(i) Less than 5 years______(ii) 5-10 years______

(ii) Above 10 years but up to 15 years__________

(iii) Above 15 years__________

(i) Typical consultancy services being offered (Please rank them in order of importance based on the consultancy fee turn over from each of them and attach your brochure if any)

1
2
3
4
5

(j) Method of charging consultancy fee (Please specify share of each in term of percentage of total turn over)

( ) Consultants man days ( )% of sales ( )% of saving ( ) % of project cost ( ) Any other (Please specify)______

(k) Mode of engagement (Please specify the share of each in term of percentage of turn over)

( ) Assignment basis ( ) Retainership basis

(2) Do you serve Small Scale Industries? (yes/No) If yes, then indicate the percentage of turn over from the SSI units.______%

(3) Please give complete name and address of 5 SSI clients along with the nature of assignment done for them

S.No.	*Name and address*	*Nature of assignment*
1		
2		
3		
4		
5		

(4) If you do not serve SSI units, please state the reasons in order of their importance.

1
2
3
4
5

(5) What are the major problems being faced by you while dealing with the SSI units? Please specify them in order of their importance.

1

2

3

4

5

(6) What do you think about usefulness of this study and how it can be made more useful? (Please attach additional sheets if you so desire).

APPENDIX-B

QUESTIONNAIRE FOR SMALL SCALE INDUSTRIAL UNITS

Part-A -Basic data

(1) Name and full address

....

(2) Year of establishment

....

(3) Constitution

....

(4) Total investment (Rs in lakhs)

....

(5) Present capacity utilization (%)

....

(6) Name, qualifications and experience of the proprietor/managing partner/managing director

....

....

....

S.No.	*Name of the organisation*	*Duration*	*Jobs handled*
1			
2			
3			
4			

(7) Have you employed any executive with degree/diploma in management? (yes/no) If yes then please provide following information.

(a) Number of executives with degree in management ———Nos.

(b) Number of executives with diploma in management———Nos.

(c) Experience profile of the executives with degree/ diploma in management.

(i) below 5 years..................(ii) 5 years but below 10 Yrs......................

(iii) 10 years but below 15 years............. (iv) 15 years and above..

Part B-Opinion of the entrepreneur

(8) Are you fully satisfied with the present level of performance (yes/no)

(9) If no, then there may be many reasons for this state of affairs both internal and external. While external reasons are mostly beyond control up to some extent, improvement could be made by minimising internal problems. Can good management practices /procedures have impact on many of the internal problems to great extent? (yes/no)

(10) If you feel that your unit is facing management problems in various functional areas, then please indicate five most important functional management problems in order of their importance.

Rank	*Problem*
I	
II	
III	
IV	
V	

(11) As you have indicated five most important management problems above, please select five

most needed management consultancy services in order of their importance which you will like to avail to solve your management problems.

Rank	*Management Consultancy needs*
I	
II	
III	
IV	
V	

(12) Have you ever utilized the services of any management consultant to solve your managerial problems? (yes/no.)

(13) If no, then what are the reasons? Some probable reasons are listed below. Please tick the reason applicable in your case. Also indicate their respective ranks depending upon the importance you attach to a particular reason.

S.No.	*Reason for not utilization of management consultancy services by SSI units*	*Rank*
1	I do not have any management problem	
2	I have in-house management expertise to solve management problems.	
3	Competent consultants are not available	
4	Available consultants are very costly.	
5	Available consultants are not suitable to my needs.	
6	Benefits from the consultancy service is less than the cost .	
7	Consultants are not reliable and will leak out information	
8	Any other(please specify).	

(14) If you have utilised the services of any management consultant in the past then please furnish following details

(i) Name and address of the consultants ....

....

(ii) Nature of the assignment......................................

(iii) Fee paid(in Rs)..

(iv) Basis of charging consultancy fee....................

....

(v) Time taken in completing the assignment ....days.

(vi) Whether all the recommendations were implemented?....................

(vii) If no then what were the reasons for not implementing the recommendations.....................

(viii) How did you come to know about your problems and the needs for the consultan...

(ix) How did you choose the consultants ....

(x) What were your original expectations from the consultant? ....

(xi) Did you specify it in ȧdvance? (yes/no).........

(xii) Did you sign any consultancy contract? (yes/no)............................

(xiii) If yes, then whether the terms and conditions of the contract were very clear? (yes/no)...............

(xiv) How far you are satisfied? please specify in percentage ....%

(xv) What were the deficiencies in the service rendered by the consultants? Please feel free while expressing your views.

S.No.	*Deficiencies in service*
1	
2	
3	
4	
5	

(xvi) What benefits accrued to you from the service vis-à-vis the consultancy fee paid?

....

(xvii) What problems did you face while utilising the services of the consultants?

....

(xviii) Will you hire the aforesaid consultant again in future?

(yes/no)..............................

(15) Do you think that the management consultants can play useful role in improving the efficiency of the SSI units? (yes/no)

(16) How much money you can spend in a year on consultancy?

(17) Is it beneficial to engage the consultants for the whole year on retainership basis on negotiated amount depending upon your payment capacity or it is better to hire them on assignment basis? (Retainership/assignment)

(18) Normally it is seen that the SSI units take the help of consultants in preparation of project /feasibility reports for loan etc. but they hardly use them after coming into production even when they are not doing well. Why it is so? Please discuss in detail.

S.No.	*Reasons for not using consultants in post production period*
1	
2	
3	
4	
5	

(19) On the one hand the SSI units are not doing well in majority of the cases, on the other hand the management consultants are hand to mouth due to lack of demand for their services. What are your suggestions for solving this paradox and for improving the utility of the management consultancy services for solving the management problems of the SSI units.

S.No.	*Suggestion*
1	
2	
3	
4	
5	
6	
7	
8	
9	
10	

20. Any other comments

APPENDIX-C

FURTHER REFERENCES FOR CONSULTATION

(1) *Accountancy*, Providing advises and financial supports (local enterprise Agency) 99: 143 January 1987.

(2) ACMA, New York, How the management consulting profession serve business enterprises 3rd Edition, New York, 1961.

(3) AIMA, New Delhi, *Research and Consultancy in Management focus on human systems*, New Delhi 1976.

(4) Alastair Bain, Presenting problem in social consultancy, three case histories concerning the selection of managers 29(7) 643-657 July 76 *Human Relations.*

(5) Alped Hunt, *The Management Consultant.* New York, Ronald Press, 1977.

(6) All India Management Association, New Delhi, *Directory of Trainers in Management.*

(7) Altier William J., Direct Involvement of clients people, *JMC* 4(4) 19-21 1988.

(8) AMACON, 1975, *Making the Most of Management Consulting Services*, New York.

(9) Amon, E. Richard and others, *Management Consultancy*, 1958.

(10) Association of Consulting Management Engineer, Committee on consulting problems and practices-ACME Survey Report on composition for professional staff in management consulting firms (excluding partner offices, directors and owners) New York, 1967.

(11) Aston, B.R, *Management Consultancy: An Instruction*, 1967.

(12) Axlim Larry, L., Hiring a consultant? *First Homework* 58(6) 39-43 Nov-Dec. 1981.

(13) Badse, A. Kaka, Planning for change (use consultant as third party facilitator), *Management Decision.* No. 4 1987, pp. 22-27.

(14) Basuki, S.N, Consultancy: Money in methods, *India Today*, 1991 Feb. 15 104-107.

(15) Batra, K.B, Project exports: Accounting Practice, *Management Accountant* 24(1) Jan. 1989 9-10.

(16) Bechhard, Richard, *The Leaders Look at the Consultative Process.*

(17) Bell, R. Chip and Leohard Nadler Hanstan (Ed), *The Client and Consultant Handbook.* (tell managers how to choose and negotiate with and get the most from the consultants.), Gulf Publishing Co. 1979.

(18) Basu, Bhuban, Management consultancy quo Nadis? *Chartered Accountant,* 1989 July 38(1) pp. 17-19.

(19) Bhattacharya, S.K. and Pinto B., Differentiating management consulting from system consulting—A general perspective, P.U. *Management Review* 1(1) Jan-June 1978.

(20) Blackford, John, Consulting for smaller companies, *Journal of Management Consultancy,* Vol. 7(1) Fall 1992 pp. 25-28.

(21) Blake R. Robert and James Srygley Montan, *Consultancy-Reading* Mass Addison Wesley 1976

(22) Brand, Shaw P., Selling consultancy services for staying in business, *The CPA Journal,* 57, pp. 99-101 Sept.. 1987.

(23) Brand, Shaw P., So you want to be a management consultant, *The CPA Journal,* 57, pp. 115-116 Nov. 1987.

(24) Brandon, J., Whose consultants fall down, *Management Today,* pp. 109-110, May 1988.

(25) Brandy J.J, Considering consultants - When outside help is justified? *Management World,* 7 March 1986 pp. 15-36.

(26) Brown, Robert G., Ten ways to get rich in consultancy by not taking to the clients, *Interface,* Vol. 9(2) Part I Feb 1979 pp. 30-36.

(27) Buddha, K.D., Consultancy services for small entrepreneurs, *Vikas Banking,* Vol. 3(1-2) Jan.-June 1983 pp. 28-36.

(28) Bushe, Gervase P. and Gibb Barrie W., Predicting organisational development consultancy competence from myers briggs type indicator and state of ego development, *Journal of Applied Behavioral Science,* Vol. 26(3) 1990 pp. 337- 357.

(29) *Business,* College of Business Administration, Georgia State University Atlanta - Small manufacturers - when going outside makes sense 39: 48-53 Jan.-Feb. -March 1989.

(30) Byrne, J.A, Before you hand out a consultant's Shingle, *Business Week,* pp. 138-9 Nov. 23, 1987.

(31) Callahan, T.F, In search of right consultants, *Association Management,* 37: 153 May 1985.

(32) Cary, James F., Management consultants as expert witness, *Journal of Management Consultancy,* Vol. 7(1) Spring 1992 pp. 52-58.

(33) Chadha, Vikram and Pritpal Singh Sandhu, Industrial Services and consultancy in Punjab- A case study, *Journal of Economic Research,* 22(2) July 1987 pp. 37-50.

(34) Charles, Maxgerson J., *Management Consultancy Services—A practical guide,* Addor Shah Grower 1988.

(35) Cooper, Owen, Technology based management consultancy, *Journal of Management Consultancy,* Vol. 7(2) Fall 1992 pp. 62-65.

(36) Correa, Carter Maria, *Use and promotion of Consultancy Ventures by Public Utilities in Latin America*, Ljubyana Center for Public Enterprises in Developing Countries, 1985.

(37) Covin Teresa Joyce and Fisher Ted V, Consultant and client must work together, Journal of *Management Consultancy*, Vol. 6(4) 1990 pp. 11-19.

(38) Culten, J.D., How to select a effective consultant, *Management Quarterly*, 19: 20-2 Oct. 1985.

(39) Davey Neil G., External Consultant- role in organisational change (*MSU Business Studies*) 1971.

(40) Dawe Philip, L. Dowling, Grahame R., Patterson and Paul G., Criteria in use to select management consultants, *Industrial Marketing Management* 1992 Aug. 21(3) pp. 183-193.

(41) Day, Ellen Banksdale and Hiram C., How to select professional services, *Industrial Marketing Management*, 1992 May 21(2) pp. 85-91.

(42) Dekon Anton K., *The Internal Consultant* (New York) American Management Association (AMA Research Study No. 101) 1969.

(43) Despande, A.R., Training of external consultants in emerging perspective in organisational development (11th National convention training by Indian Society for Training and Development New Delhi at Bhopal from 26th Oct. to 28th Oct. 1980).

(44) Devidson, J.P., Management consultants—are they really supervisors? *Security Management*, 30: 79: 9 March 1986.

(45) Dick, Robert F., When and how to use management consultants in marketing job? - Responsibility of top man and his staff Edited by Elizabeth Martin, Bombay, Taraporavala and Co.

(46) Dixit, P.P., Small Consultants survival Kit, *Journal*

of Management Consultancy, Vol. 4(4) 1988, pp. 40-43.

(47) *Economist,* Accountant consultants thyself (consultancy series) 308, 89-90 Sept. 1988.

(48) *Economist,* Outside looking in a survey of management consultancy (Spl. Report) 306, June 1-18 F13'88.

(49) Egerton Henery and Teremy Becon, *Consultants: Selection, Use and Appraisal* (National Industrial Conference Board) New York, 1970.

(50) Eisenhert, T., Pros and cons of hiring a consultant (Corporate identify consultants), *Business Marketing* 74:33 Jan. 1989.

(51) Elotrolt, John B., Procedure for improving the evaluation of SBDC consulting activities, *Journal of Small Business Management,* 25 (1) pp. 67-71.

(52) ESCAP 1983, *Consultancy Services available in Developing ESCAP countries,* United Nations NY.

(53) Farrell, J.W., Choosing and using consultants (logistic consultants), *Traffic Management,* 26 "80"2 July 1987.

(54) Federation of Indian Export Organisation; *(FIEO)* New Delhi: Consultancy Exports from India.

(55) *Financial Express* (Ed.), Needless fear, 6 March 1987 P-5.

(56) Fisher, A.B., The ever bigger boom in consulting, *Fortune,* 119. 113 April (24, 1989).

(57) Fitzgerld, Thomas H, OD Practitioner in the business world, Theory vs Reality, *Organisational Dynamics,* 16 (1) 20-23 Summer 1987.

(58) Forbes, Wallace F. and Rosen Bloom Arther H., Shield for Director- The outside consultant, *Management Review,* AMA, New York 66 (12), 26-28, 37-39. Dec. 1977.

(59) Forsyth, Patrick, Marketing consultancy services, *Management Accounting* 69 (4), 42-43.

(60) Frankeknhuis Jean Pierrae, How to get a good consultant, *Harvard Business Review* 55 (6), 133-139 Nov-Dec. 1997.

(61) Freeman C., Using consultant to solve quality problems, *Business,* 37:50-4 July-August-Sept. 1987.

(62) Fritz Steele, 1975. Consulting for organisational change Amherst University of Masachusette Press, 1975.

(63) Fulton, R.L, Let us consultant consult organisation must manage, *Training* 22, 47-50. Sept. 1985.

(64) Ganesh, S.R, Organisational consultants: A comparison of style, *Human Relations,* 31 (1) 1-28 Jan. 1978.

(65) Getz, L.V, Expand your practice to provide Business Advisory Service, *Practical Accountant* 18: 79-82.

(66) Goodstein, Leonard Devid, Consulting with human services systems, Reading Mass Addition, Wesley Pub. Co. 1978. Great Britain National Economic Officer Business Efficiency: An ABC of Advisory Service, London H.M. Stationery Office, 1968.

(67) Gramer, L.E and Metzger R.O, *Consulting in Management,* Englewood Cliffs N.J, Prentice Hall 1983.

(68) Grawer, R. Getting tab off Granm-Rud man, Consultants interpreting Act, April 21, 1986-*Business Week,* Hightstan NJ.

(69) Grinstain, G., A client's eye view of consulting, *JMC* 4 (2) 1988 pp. 36.

(70) Guss, L.M, Marketing consultants when and how to select and use, *Handbook of Modern Marketing* ed. By Victor B. Bnell, New York, Mcgraw Hill, 1986.

(71) Haggarty A.G., Picking a management consultant- No easy task, *National Underwriter,* 89:30: Jan 21 1985.

(72) Hal, Higdon, *The Business Healers,* New York, Random House, 1969.

(73) Hall, R.Duane, Intricacies of people problems approach, *JMC* 4 (4) P-23-31 1988.

(74) Hankinson, Alan, Small firms: The consultancy barrier, *Management Accounting* (UK) 1990 May 68 (5) 56-58.

(75) *Harvard Business Review* 55 (4) 84-92 July-August 1977, Rate yourself as a client.

(76) Hibbert, Chelvin, *Client/Consultants Managing a large interventions from People and Organisation* Ed. By Andrew Kakabadee, Allershot Gower, 1982.

(77) Hollander Stanley C., Business consultants and client—A literature research on the marketing practices and problem of management research and advisory professionals.

(78) Hollander, Stanley C, *Management Consultant and Clients.*

(79) Horringa, Dirk, Consulting across the grave, *JMC,* 7 (3) 1993 Spring P-35-36.

(80) Huczynski Andrzej A., *Management Guru: What makes them? How to become one?* London Rcztledse 1993.

(81) Hunt, Alfred, *The Management Consultants,* Ronald Press, New York 1977.

(82) Hupp, Bwer, This remarkably stable profession, *JMC* 4(2) pp. 21-25, 1988.

(83) ICICI 1973, Consultancy Services in India- On background paper. (Seminar on consultancy services in India, Bombay, 1972).

(84) India Investment Centre 1976, *Consultancy and Contract Engineering Organisations—A guide for selection of consultancy organisations,* New Delhi 1976.

(85) India Investment Centre 1982, *India Offer Consultancy,* New Delhi, 1982.

(86) *Industrial Times,* Management consultancy shifting organisation from cheft. 20(14) 10-15 July 3-16, 1978.

(87) Kahri, Robert, Ethics of contingent fees, values, billing and commission *JMC* 7(1) P-24-25 1992.

(88) Kanfma, M., Who should be running the officer? You or export? The Office Stanford 102, 172-3 July 1985.

(89) Kelly, K., Buying a consultant's expertise, Executive female (national association for female executives New York) 8, 17-20 Jan-F 85.

(90) Kenneth, J. Albert, *How to be Your Own Management Consultant,* McGraw Hill Book Co., New York, 1978.

(91) Kerr, James, Company Directors at work, *Director* 34(7) 26-27 Jan 1982.

(92) Kharbande, O.P, Management consultancy on the verse of Take off. *Director Digest* 17(4) Jan-Feb 1987 80-87.

(93) Kirmani, Syeed S. and Bauss Warnen C., *Consulting Professionals in Developing Countries*—A strategy for development, World Bank, Washington DC 1992.

(94) Klein, P., Outside resources—key to development *Management Review,* AMA, New York, 74:36-9 July 1985.

(95) Knox, S., Advice and consultant Blare Future price 16, 90-2D'85.

(96) Kuppachi, Rama Murthy, Managing by Consultation—*A Gobal and Asian Experience,* New Delhi, Sagen 2.

(97) Lal, Lalit, Buying professional services—An examination of some key variable in the selection process, *Material Manager,* Sept-Oct. 1990 10(5).

(98) Leibowitz, M.R, Consultants: Who needs them? Electronics firms it seems. *Electric Business* 14, 112 + N:1988.

(99) Lie Lwan H. and Russel Tausig, *Productivity through consultancy in small industrial enterprises,* Asian Productivity Organisation (APO), Tokyo 1974.

(100) Line, A.H and Metz C.K.G,. Managing Management Services, London, Industrial Commercial Techniques Ltd. 1972.

(101) Lippit, Gordan and Lippit Ronard, *The Consulting Process in Action,* La-Jolla Calif University Association, 1978.

(102) Maisten Devid M., Balancing the Professional services firms sloan, *Mgt. Review* 24(1) 15-19 Fall 1982.

(103) Magnet, M., Who needs a trend spotter? *Fortune* 112, 51 2+D 9'85.

(104) Management Development Institute, New Delhi, *Technical Consultancy Services established by financial institution—An analytical study,* New Delhi 1982.

(105) *Management Today,* London England, Use and Abuses of consultants, pp. 72-4 F 1986.

(106) Maviwalba, K.D., Consulting services in the public sector-A perspective view, *SCOPE,* New Delhi.

(107) Marston, Ronald C, Management expertise—its application in developing countries, *Personnel Administer,* 22(8) 54-56 August 1978.

(108) Nastin, J., Doing business in Japan—a personal view of a Canadian management consultant, *Business Quarterly.*

(109) Maulder, Mark and others, Systematic appraisal

of leadership effectiveness of consultants, *Human Relations* 36(11) 1045-1064 Nov. 1983.

(110) MCGivern, C.K and Finaman S, *Research and Consultancy—toward a conceptional synthesis,* 20(4) 425-439 Oct. 1993.

(111) M. C. Givern Chris, *Some aspects of the relationship between consultants and clients in organisation* 20(3) 367-386 July 83.

(112) Metzger, R.O., Guidelines for tomorrow consultants *JMC* 4(4) 1988 P13-18.

(113) Mishra, C., Pricing in consultancy, *Indian Journal of Marketing* 17(1) 17-20 Sept. 1986.

(114) Moses Irudianathan, *Consultancy Services available in the U.S, Canada and India.* Administrative Staff College of India 1977.

(115) Mrmenakes, A.A. and Burdy, H.B, Consultation Research: Contribution to practice and direction for improvement, *Journal of Management*. p. 361: 5: 14: 339-65 Jan 88.

(116) Mukharjee D.N, Selling advice: Foreign consultancy firms are making entry into India, *Business World,* 1992 Oct. 21-Nov. 3 12(15).

(117) Nadganda, P.M., Govt. and public sector organisation and consultancy services, *Indian Highways* 10(12) 120-122 Dec. 1982.

(118) Nadkarni, G.A, *Management Consultancy in performance productivity and profit improvement,* Bombay 1976.

(119) *Nation Business,* 76; 28 S'FF, Hiring a consultant for family firm.

(120) Natrajan, R., India needs management consultancy, *Integrated Management,* March 1975 pp. 5-6.

(121) Navedini M, Developing controls in 1990: The growing role of consultant, *Building* 65; 32: March 1991.

(122) Nees Danielle B. and Greivies Larry E., Seeing behind the look like management consultants, *Organisational Dynamics,* American Mgt. Association 68-69 Winter 1985.

(123) Nufrio, Phillip M., Diary of mad internal consultant, *Group and Organisational Studies,* 8(1) 7-18 March 1983.

(124) Overholt, Miles H and Altier William J., Participative process consulting the hard and soft of it, *JMC* 4(3) 1988 P13-23.

(125) Padem Devid L, Consulting on scholarly activity: Rationale and references, *JMC* 7(3) 1993 Spring p. 45.

(126) Paxton, J., Help! I can't do it alone, *Personnel Jr.* 64 58-9 July 1985.

(127) Payne A, Effective use of professional management services, *Management Decision* 24, No. 6 16-24 1986.

(128) Perham, J.C., The shirt sleeve consultant (overcoming distant of management consultant), *Business Month,* 125, 52-4 Jan. 1985.

(129) *Personnel Management,* A change in contract style for consultancy Job? 17:59 May 1985.

(130) Peter Rosik, Four ways to profit from consultants *HR Magazine* Nov 37 (11), 1992 77-87.

(131) Poe, R. Calling in the experts (Franchise consultants) *Venture* 10:48 March 1988.

(132) Prete, Maurizio Boschettie Carlo: Corporate planner as consultant, *Long Range Planning* 23(6) 23-30 Prabandh.

(133) Price Charlton R. Professional Development worldwide view, *JMC* 4(1) pp. 43-46 1989.

(134) Putnam, Arnold O., Challenges to the profession, *JMC* 5(2) pp. 19-24.

(135) Putnam Arnold D., Excellence is not enough, *JMC* 4(3) 1988 pp. 6-12.

(136) Radic Zrenimir, Consultancy in the model of complementary technological development in the world, *Indian Management* 28(1) Jan. 1989 pp. 23-33.

(137) Raine Ronald V., How to get max value from consultants. *Administrator* 22(1) 30-33.

(138) Rerose, J.F, When to use a development consultant (Joint venture Project) 24, 18-19 Je. 88 Pension World 6255 Barfield Rd., Atlanta GA 30328.

(139) Richard F., Amen and others, *Management Consultancy* 1958.

(140) Roger Bennett, *Choosing and Using Management Consultant*, London Kogan Page, 1990.

(141) Ron Tepper, *Becoming a top consultant how the expert do it*, New York 1985.

(142) Roxin, Charles L., Choosing a TXM consultant, *Trg. and Dev. Journal* 1992 Feb. 46(2) 69-76.

(143) Roy Namratha, Consultancy whose need is it anyway, *Indian Journal of Trg. and Development*, 1992 Nov-Dec. 22(6) pp. 37-39.

(144) Royese, William, *Becoming a Top Consultant: How the expert do it*, New York 1985.

(145) Sanghi, A.R, Consultancy in small and medium industries, *Consultancy Methodology and Styles* Ed. N. Singh Management Consultants Association of India, Mumbai, pp. 95-101.

(146) Schaffer, Robert H., Advice to internal and external consultants—expand your client's capacity to use your help, *Journal of Advance Management* 41(4) 39-42 Autamn 1976.

(147) Schaffer (Robert H.) and Michanlgen Keith E., Incremental strategy for consulting success, *JMC*(2) pp. 8-14 1989.

(148) Scheren John, Making stride, A model to help your

client create breakthrough, *JMC* 7(3) 1993 Spring pp. 7-10.

(149) Scholz, Karl Adolf, Worldwide outlook for professionals, *JMC* (5) (1) 1989 pp. 10-13.

(150) Shapiro, Eileen C. Eecles, Robert G. Soske Trinal, Consulting -has the solution become part of the problem? 1993 *Sum* 34 (4) 89-95.

(151) Shays, E. Michall, Straight talk about management consulting, *JMC* 4(3) pp. 28-30 1988.

(152) Shay, Philip W., 1964- How to get best results from management consultants, AMCE, New York.

(153) Shenson, H.L., Payment for performance (working with client for performance fee) *Nation Business* 79, 52 R April 1991. U.S Chamber of Commerce.

(154) Shenson, Howard L., Unhappy client: Who is to blame? *JMC* 6 (4) pp. 38-41, 1990.

(155) Shiva Rama S., Consultancy and project exports-over sea entry strategy, *Foreign Trade Review*, July-Sept. 1992 27 (2) 143-158.

(156) Singh, Arinudh and Tyagi, A.K, Strategy for consultancy services marketing *Business and environment in India* Ed. By Ahmad S and Ahmad K., New Delhi, Ashish Publishing House, 1990.

(157) Stanely Clande Maxwell, The consulting engineer presenting the professional and management problems involved in the practice of consulting engineering, New York, Welsay, 1961.

(158) Stephanek, Joseph E. 1962—*Small Industry Advisory Services- An International study* (Stanford Research Institute-International Industrial Development Centre).

(159) Stptran, Timewell, How consultants consults? *Banker* 1993 April 143 (806) 22-25.

(160) Stroh P, Purposeful consulting, *Organisational Dynamics* 16, 49-67 Autumn, 1987.

(161) Stuller J. Crives, *Consultancy—A Growing Damned Across the Board*, New York 25, 51, May 1988.

(162) Tagirui, Renato, Training and managing of consultants, *JMC* 7(1) pp. 3-8 1992 Spring.

(163) Taneja, Shiv and Sleavia George, Champions of change, *Business Today*, Sept. 22-Oct. 6, 1993 2(18) 63-73.

(164) Tatham, Leura, *The Efficiency Experts an Impartial Survey of Management Consulting*, Business Publication, 1964.

(165) Thomas, Hedley, *Management consulting around the World* 7 (1) pp. 26-27 1992 Spring.

(166) Timewell, Stephen, How consultants consult: *The Banker*, 1993 April 143 (806) 22-25.

(167) *Training and Development Journal*, Four by four. The Art of Choosing a Consultant 1992 Jan. 46 (1) 21-26.

(168) UNIDO 1968, *Manual on Use of Consultants in Developing countries*, New York.

(169) *Vikas Banking*, Role of consultants is development banks 3 (1&2) 37-42 Jan-June 1983.

(170) Walley, Brain Halferd, *Management Services Hand Book*, London, Business Books, 1973.

(171) Walsh John Edward, *Guidelines for Management Consultants on Asia*, Asian Productivity Organisation 1973, Tokyo.

(172) Washburn, Stewart, A Let's call it asset based marketing, *JMC* 6(4) 1990 pp. 4-10.

(173) Wates, Berfram G., How to market a consulting practice, *JMC* 4(3) 1988 pp. 53-58.

(174) Wheatley, Watter J. and Armstrong Terry R, Beware of the uncertain client, *JMC* 4(3) 1988 pp. 33-38.

(175) Whitrside, Conon Doyle, 1969, *Accountant's Guide to Professional Management Advisory Services*, Prentice Hall, Englewood Cliffs, N.J.

(176) William, W.E, Choose me "Entrepreneur choose consultant, *Venture*, New York 10:16 May 1988.

(177) Wiley Yark Hohn, *Consultation: A Book of Readings* 1975 Dinkomeyer Con and Carlon.

(178) Wilson, Seney, *Effective Use of Business Consultants*—a research study and report prepared for New York, Financial Executive Research Foundation, 1964.